NUTRIBULLET RECIPE BOOK

Energizing Juices and Smoothies for a Balanced Life

JULIET O. WELCH

Copyright © 2024 By LIZZIE K. BAILEY. All rights reserved worldwide.

No part of this book may be reproduced or transmitted in any form or by any means, electronic or mechanical, including photocopying, recording, or by any information storage and retrieval system, without written permission from the publisher, except for the inclusion of brief quotations in a review.

Warning-Disclaimer:

The purpose of this book is to educate and entertain. The author or publisher does not guarantee that anyone following the techniques, suggestions, tips, ideas, or strategies will become successful. The author and publisher shall have neither liability nor responsibility to anyone with respect to any loss or damage caused, or alleged to be caused, directly or indirectly, by the information contained in this book.

This copyright notice and disclaimer apply to the entirety of the book and its contents, whether in print or electronic form, and extend to all future editions or revisions of the book. Unauthorized use or reproduction of this book or its contents is strictly prohibited and may result in legal action.

TABLE OF CONTENTS

INTRODUCTION 8

Brief Overview of the NutriBullet and its benefits 9
Importance of incorporating healthy ingredients into daily meals 10
Tips for using the NutriBullet for optimal results 11
NutriBullet Basics 12
Understanding the NutriBullet machine 13
Tips for selecting fresh and highquality ingredients 15
Nutrient retention through blending techniques 16

CHAPTER 1: SMOOTHIES 18

Strawberry Banana Smoothie 18
Orange Julius Smoothie 18
Very Berry Smoothie 19
Peaches and Cream Smoothie 19
Chocolate Peanut Butter Smoothie 20
Green Smoothie 20
Tropical Smoothie 21
Blueberry Almond Smoothie 21
Peach Mango Smoothie 22
Acai Berry Smoothie 22
Pomegranate Smoothie 23
Watermelon Lime Smoothie 23
Grapefruit Spinach Smoothie 24
Cherry Vanilla Smoothie 24
Pineapple Coconut Smoothie 25

CHAPTER 2: BREAKFASTS 26

Nutribullet Pancakes 26

Breakfast Power Bowl 26
Banana Oatmeal Smoothie Bowl 27
Peach Parfait Smoothie Bowl 27
Berry Yogurt Bowl 27
Pumpkin Pie Oatmeal 28
Blueberry Muffin Smoothie Bowl 28
Frittata in a Mug 29
Spinach and Tomato Scramble 29
Tropical Fruit Salad 30
Overnight Chia Oats 30
Nutribullet Omelet 31
Breakfast Burrito Bowl 31
Breakfast Quinoa with Berries 32

CHAPTER 3: APPETIZERS AND SNACKS 33

Nutribullet Hummus 33
Guacamole 33
Nutribullet Salsa 34
Kale Pesto 34
Coconut Whipped Cream 35
Nut and Seed Trail Mix 35
Energy Bites 36
Green Goddess Dip 36
Roasted Red Pepper Dip 37
Spinach and Artichoke Dip 37
Nutribullet Salad Dressings 38
Tzatziki Sauce 38
Fruit Smoothie Popsicles 39
Chocolate Banana Popsicles 39

CHAPTER 4: SOUPS AND STEWS 41

Velvety Butternut Squash Soup 41

Creamy Broccoli Cheddar Soup 41

Classic Tomato Basil Soup 42

Comforting Carrot Ginger Soup 42

Creamy Potato Leek Soup 43

Roasted Cauliflower Soup 44

Lentil Stew 44

Minestrone Soup 45

Thai Coconut Curry Soup 46

Black Bean Soup 46

Creamy Mushroom Soup 47

Italian Wedding Soup 48

Chicken Noodle Soup 48

Roasted Red Pepper Soup 49

CHAPTER 5: SAUCES AND SPREADS 50

Simple Tomato Sauce 50

Alfredo Sauce 50

Basil Pesto 51

Cilantro Lime Crema 51

BBQ Sauce 52

Tahini Sauce 52

Olive Tapenade 53

Sundried Tomato Spread 53

Marinara Sauce 54

Peanut Sauce 54

Mango Chutney 55

Coconut Curry Sauce 55

Cranberry Sauce 56

Maple Dijon Vinaigrette 56

CHAPTER 6: NUT AND SEED BUTTERS..58

Almond Butter 58
Cashew Butter 58
Sunflower Seed Butter 58
Chocolate Hazelnut Butter 59
Cookie Dough Almond Butter 59
Strawberry Almond Butter 60
Pumpkin Seed Butter 60
Cinnamon Walnut Butter 61
Maple Pecan Butter 61
Coconut Butter 61
Peanut Butter 62
Tahini 62
Chai Spiced Walnut Butter 63
Chocolate Almond Butter 63

CHAPTER 7: DESSERTS 65

Almond Butter Bites 65
Chocolate Avocado Mousse 65
Coconut Macaroons 66
Chocolate Banana Protein Muffins 66
Black Bean Brownies 67
Mango Sorbet 67
Banana "Ice Cream" 68
Pumpkin Pie Smoothie 68
Strawberry Sorbet 69
Peanut Butter Banana "Ice Cream" 69
Chia Seed Pudding 69
Blueberry Crumble 70
Dark Chocolate Bark 70

Nut Butter Fudge 71

CHAPTER 8: MEAT AND BOWLS 72

Thai Quinoa Salad 72

TexMex Rice Bowl 72

Chicken Fajita Bowl 72

Shrimp and Avocado Salad Bowl 73

Taco Salad Bowl 73

Curried Chickpea Salad Bowl 74

Vegan Chili 75

Lentil Bolognese 75

Veggie Fried Rice Bowl 76

Burrito Bowl 76

Poke Bowl 77

Harvest Bowl 77

Tofu Scramble Bowl 78

Mediterranean Quinoa Salad 79

CHAPTER 9: DRINKS 80

Nutribullet Milkshakes 80

Fruit Smoothies 80

Green Juice 80

Nutribullet Lattes 81

Matcha Latte 81

Pumpkin Spice Latte 82

Iced Mocha Latte 82

Golden Milk Turmeric Latte 83

Hot Chocolate 83

Chai Latte 83

Strawberry Banana Smoothie 84

Peanut Butter Banana Protein Shake 84

Blueberry Almond Smoothie *85*

Watermelon Juice *85*

Orange Juice *86*

CHAPTER 10: NUTRIBULLET TIPS AND RESOURCES 87

Variations for Dietary Needs 89

Keeping it Simple 90

Portion Sizes 91

Choosing Your Ingredients 92

Adding Protein and Fiber 93

Blending Tips 94

Smoothie Prep and Storage Ideas 94

Creative Vessels and Toppings 95

Tips 96

Cleaning the Nutribullet 97

Top Resources and Websites 98

CONCLUSION 99

INTRODUCTION

Welcome to the Nutribullet Recipe Book your comprehensive guide to unlocking the full power of your Nutribullet blender! As a Nutribullet owner myself, I'm excited to share the incredible benefits and delicious possibilities this amazing appliance can bring to your daily life.

The Nutribullet is more than just a blender it's a nutrition extraction system that transforms whole foods into nutrientrich smoothies, soups, nut butters, and so much more. By breaking down the cellular walls of fruits, vegetables, seeds, and nuts, the highpowered Nutribullet is able to extract all the vitamins, minerals, and antioxidants your body craves. This means you get to enjoy all the goodness of wholesome, unprocessed foods in an easytodigest liquid form.

Incorporating the Nutribullet into your routine is one of the simplest and most effective ways to boost your overall health and wellness. Instead of settling for processed, sugarladen foods and beverages, you can start your day with a nourishing smoothie packed with fresh produce, healthy fats, and plantbased proteins. The balanced nutrition from these Nutribullet creations will leave you feeling energized, satisfied, and empowered to make better choices throughout your day.

In this recipe book, you'll find a wide variety of delicious and nutritious options to try, from classic fruit smoothies to savory soups and creamy nut butters. Whether you're looking to lose weight, increase your energy levels, or simply improve your diet, the Nutribullet can help you achieve your goals. The recipes are easy to follow, use affordable everyday ingredients, and can be customized to suit your unique taste preferences and dietary needs.

Beyond the recipes, you'll also find helpful tips and tricks for getting the most out of your Nutribullet. From choosing the best produce to mastering blending techniques, this book will equip you with the knowledge and confidence to take your nutrition to the next level. You'll learn how to build a balanced, nutrientdense smoothie, store your creations for maximum freshness, and introduce more wholesome foods into your family's meals.

So get ready to unlock a world of culinary possibilities and experience the transformative power of the Nutribullet. With this recipe book as your guide, you'll be well on your way to a happier, healthier you. Let's get blending!

Brief Overview of the NutriBullet and its benefits

In a world filled with fad diets and gimmicky health gadgets, the NutriBullet stands out as a true gamechanger when it comes to transforming your approach to wellness. This compact and userfriendly highspeed blender has taken the health and nutrition space by storm, empowering millions of people to take control of their wellbeing through the power of nutrientdense whole foods.

At its core, the NutriBullet is designed to make it easier than ever to incorporate more fruits, vegetables, greens, nuts, seeds, and other superfoods into your daily routine. Through its patented nutrient extraction technology, the NutriBullet is able to break down the cellular walls of these whole food ingredients, releasing all of their vital vitamins, minerals, antioxidants, and phytonutrients. This allows your body to absorb the maximum nutritional benefits in the most efficient way possible.

Compared to traditional blenders that simply puree ingredients, the NutriBullet goes a step further by turning even the toughest whole foods, like kale and almonds, into a smooth and creamy liquid that's simple for your body to digest. This makes it possible to consume a far more concentrated dose of nutrients in one sitting, without having to chew through bulky servings of fruits and veggies.

But the NutriBullet's benefits extend far beyond just nutrition. This versatile appliance also makes it remarkably easy to prepare a wide variety of healthy and delicious meals, snacks, and beverages from refreshing smoothies and creamy soups to flavorful dips and nut butters. And with its compact, countertopfriendly design and userfriendly onebutton operation, the NutriBullet fits seamlessly into even the busiest of lifestyles.

Perhaps most importantly, the NutriBullet has the power to transform the way you approach your overall health and wellness. By making it simpler to regularly consume a concentrated dose of nature's most nourishing whole foods, the NutriBullet can help support immunity, boost energy levels, aid digestion, promote weight management, and so much more. Many NutriBullet users, myself included, have experienced remarkable improvements in their physical and mental wellbeing after making this powerful blender a part of their daily routine.

Whether your goal is to drop a few pounds, manage a chronic health condition, or simply develop healthier eating habits, the NutriBullet can be an invaluable ally on your wellness journey. Its unique ability to extract the maximum nutrition from whole food ingredients, combined with its versatility and ease of use, make it one of the most impactful kitchen appliances you can invest in for the sake of your longterm health.

So if you're ready to take a more proactive, plantbased approach to fueling your body, I highly encourage you to explore the incredible benefits of the NutriBullet. With this compact yet powerful blender by your side, achieving your wellness goals has never been simpler or more delicious.

Importance of incorporating healthy ingredients into daily meals

In today's fastpaced, conveniencedriven world, it's all too easy to fall into the trap of relying on processed, nutrientpoor foods to fuel our bodies. Whether it's grabbing a quick takeout meal, snacking on bags of chips, or chugging down sugary energy drinks, these types of foods may provide a temporary energy boost or satisfaction, but they often lack the vital nutrients our bodies need to truly thrive.

The truth is, our modern diets have become alarmingly devoid of the wholesome, nutrientdense ingredients that our ancestors once relied on for nourishment. Things like fresh fruits and vegetables, whole grains, nuts, seeds, and other plantbased superfoods have been largely replaced by heavily refined, artificial, and caloriedense processed foods. And this dietary shift has come with a heavy price rising rates of obesity, heart disease, diabetes, and other chronic health conditions that are closely linked to poor nutrition.

But it doesn't have to be this way. By making a conscious effort to incorporate more whole, minimallyprocessed foods into our daily meals and snacks, we have the power to dramatically transform our health and wellbeing. These nutrientdense ingredients are quite literally bursting with the vitamins, minerals, antioxidants, fiber, and other beneficial plant compounds that our bodies need to function optimally.

Take leafy greens, for example. Foods like kale, spinach, and Swiss chard are packed with essential nutrients like vitamins A, C, and K, as well as minerals like calcium, iron, and magnesium. They also contain powerful antioxidants that can help neutralize harmful free radicals and reduce inflammation in the body. And when you break down those tough cell walls through highspeed blending, you can unlock an even greater concentration of those vital nutrients.

The same goes for fruits, vegetables, nuts, seeds, and other whole food ingredients. Each one offers its own unique nutritional profile, providing your body with a diverse array of phytochemicals, fiber, healthy fats, and other compounds that work synergistically to support optimal health. And by crowding your diet with these nutrientdense foods, you naturally crowd out the less nutritious, processed items that can contribute to weight gain, disease, and a general feeling of unwellness.

Of course, I know it's not always easy to prioritize whole, homemade meals in our busy, onthego lifestyles. That's where tools like the NutriBullet become invaluable. By making it quick, easy, and delicious to incorporate more fruits, vegetables, greens, and other superfoods into your daily routine, the NutriBullet takes a lot of the guesswork and effort out of healthy eating. With just a few simple ingredients and a quick spin in the blender, you can create nutrientpacked smoothies, soups, spreads, and more that provide your body with a powerful dose of nourishment.

Ultimately, the importance of prioritizing whole, minimallyprocessed foods in your diet cannot be overstated. These natural, nutrientdense ingredients have the power to transform your health on a cellular level, boosting your energy, supporting your immune system, improving your digestion, and so much more. And with the help of a tool like the NutriBullet, making these wholesome foods a regular part of your lifestyle has never been simpler or more delicious.

Tips for using the NutriBullet for optimal results

As revolutionary as the NutriBullet is, it's important to understand that simply owning one isn't enough to reap all of its incredible health benefits. To truly maximize the nutrient extraction power of this appliance and see the best results, there are a few key tips and techniques that are worth mastering.

First and foremost, it's crucial to select highquality, nutrientdense ingredients when using your NutriBullet. This means focusing on whole food items like fresh or frozen fruits and vegetables, leafy greens, nuts, seeds, and other superfoods and steering clear of processed, sugary, or unhealthy additives. The NutriBullet is designed to extract the maximum nutrition from these natural, plantbased ingredients, so be sure to choose the best quality produce you can find, ideally organic when possible.

It's also important to master the proper blending technique for your NutriBullet. Start by adding your liquid ingredients to the cup first, as this helps ensure thorough blending. Then layer in your leafy greens, fruits, nuts, and any other solid ingredients. Be sure to secure the blade attachment tightly, and then blend on the highest speed setting until you achieve a smooth, uniform consistency. If needed, use the handy tamper tool to gently push the ingredients down toward the blades, being careful not to overcrowd the cup.

Timing is another crucial factor when using the NutriBullet. As a general rule of thumb, you'll want to avoid blending for longer than one minute at a time. The powerful highspeed blades generate a significant amount of friction, which can cause the ingredients to heat up and build up internal pressure, especially in a sealed NutriBullet cup. Blending for extended periods can lead to leakage, splattering, or even the contents exploding out of the container when opened. To prevent this, stick to blending in 60second intervals, giving the motor a chance to cool down in between.

It's also worth noting that the NutriBullet is not intended for blending hot ingredients. Attempting to make hot soups or other warm mixtures directly in the NutriBullet cups can be extremely dangerous, as the builtup pressure and heat can cause serious injury. Instead, blend room temperature or chilled ingredients first, and then transfer the mixture to a stovetop pot to heat through.

Finally, pay close attention to how you store your NutriBullet creations. Avoid leaving any blended items whether smoothies, nut butters, or sauces sealed in the cups for extended periods, as the trapped gases from fermentation can lead to dangerous pressure buildup. It's best to either consume your blended goods immediately, or transfer them to a different storage container before refrigerating.

By keeping these tips in mind and mastering the basic techniques, you'll be well on your way to getting the absolute most out of your NutriBullet. With a little practice, this powerful appliance will become an invaluable tool in your health and wellness arsenal, empowering you to unlock the incredible nutritional potential of whole foods like never before.

NutriBullet Basics

At its core, the NutriBullet is a revolutionary highspeed blender designed to transform the way we consume whole, nutrientdense foods. Unlike traditional blenders that simply puree ingredients, the NutriBullet utilizes a unique extraction process to break down the cellular walls and release the maximum nutritional content of fruits, vegetables, greens, nuts, seeds and other superfoods.

This impressive nutrient extraction is made possible by the NutriBullet's powerful 6001200 watt motor, which spins the stainless steel blade at an incredible speed of up to 25,000 RPM. This highvelocity blending action pulverizes even the toughest whole food ingredients, turning them into a smooth, creamy and highly absorbable liquid.

The end result is a nutrientpacked "superfood smoothie" that provides your body with a concentrated dose of vitamins, minerals, antioxidants, fiber and other beneficial plant compounds. These nutrients are now in a form that's incredibly easy for your digestive system to readily absorb and utilize, giving you an unparalleled nutritional boost in every sip.

Beyond its impressive nutrient extraction capabilities, the NutriBullet also stands out for its incredible versatility and userfriendliness. With a compact, countertopfriendly design and simple onebutton operation, this appliance makes it easy for anyone to whip up a wide variety of healthy, whole foodbased dishes from refreshing smoothies and creamy soups to flavorful nut butters and homemade sauces.

And with a range of cup sizes and specialized accessories available, the NutriBullet can be adapted to suit your individual needs, whether you're blending up a quick singleserve smoothie or preparing a familysized batch of nutrientdense goodness.

Of course, getting the most out of your NutriBullet goes beyond simply owning the appliance it's also about selecting the right ingredients and mastering the proper blending techniques. When choosing foods to blend, focus on incorporating a balanced mix of leafy greens, fresh or frozen fruits, nuts, seeds and other nutrientdense whole food items. Opting for organic produce when possible, and limiting highsugar, highfat additives, will ensure you're creating blends that are brimming with nourishing plantbased compounds.

It's also crucial to follow the recommended blending instructions, starting with liquids first and using the tamper tool to gently guide ingredients toward the blade if needed. Avoiding overblending, and never attempting to blend hot items directly in the sealed NutriBullet cups, will help prevent potential leaks, splatters or explosive pressure buildup.

With a little bit of practice, you'll be whipping up delectable and amazingly nutritious NutriBullet creations in no time. This compact yet powerful appliance truly has the potential to revolutionize the way you approach your health and wellness, making it easier than ever to crowd your diet with an abundance of whole, plantbased foods.

Understanding the NutriBullet machine

At first glance, the NutriBullet may seem like just another runofthemill blender but a deeper dive into its innovative design and engineering quickly reveals why this compact appliance is so much more than meets the eye.

The key to the NutriBullet's unparalleled performance lies in its powerful 6001200 watt motor, which provides the driving force behind its industryleading nutrient extraction capabilities. This hightorque motor is engineered to spin the stainless steel blade at an incredible speed of up to 25,000 RPM, generating the intense friction and cyclonic action needed to transform even the toughest whole food ingredients into a smooth, creamy liquid.

But the NutriBullet's motor is just one part of the equation. The appliance's unique blade design also plays a crucial role in maximizing nutrient extraction. Unlike standard blender blades that simply chop and puree, the NutriBullet's blade is strategically angled and serrated to slice, grind and crush ingredients with surgical precision. This allows it to thoroughly break down the cellular walls of foods like leafy greens, carrots, nuts and seeds unlocking a far greater concentration of vitamins, minerals, antioxidants and other beneficial plant compounds.

The compact, countertopfriendly size of the NutriBullet is another key aspect of its genius design. By keeping the overall footprint small and easy to store, the brand has made it remarkably simple for healthconscious consumers to integrate this powerful blender into even the most spaceconstrained kitchens. And with a sleek, modern aesthetic that complements any decor, the NutriBullet looks right at home on the countertop, serving as a constant reminder and motivator to maintain healthy eating habits.

Perhaps most impressively, the NutriBullet has managed to pack all of this highperformance blending technology into an incredibly userfriendly interface. With a simple onebutton operation and intuitive assembly, this appliance makes it easy for anyone regardless of their cooking experience to create delicious and nutritious whole foodbased smoothies, soups, nut butters and more.

Even the accessories that come with the NutriBullet have been meticulously designed to enhance the user experience. The various cup sizes, lids, blades and tamper tools are all engineered to work in seamless harmony, ensuring optimal results with minimal effort. And the fact that these accessories are dishwashersafe further adds to the NutriBullet's convenience factor, taking the hassle out of cleanup.

Ultimately, the genius of the NutriBullet lies in its ability to make nutrientdense whole foods more accessible and enjoyable for the average consumer. By stripping away the time, effort and intimidation often associated with healthy eating, this appliance empowers people of all ages and dietary preferences to take a more proactive, plantbased approach to fueling their bodies.

Whether you're a seasoned health nut or simply looking to revamp your nutrition, the NutriBullet's cuttingedge design and engineering ensure that nourishing your body with nature's most vitalityboosting ingredients has never been easier or more enjoyable. With this compact yet powerful appliance by your side, the path to vibrant, wholebody wellness has never been clearer.

Tips for selecting fresh and highquality ingredients

When it comes to getting the absolute most out of your NutriBullet, the quality and freshness of the ingredients you use is paramount. After all, this powerful appliance is designed to extract the maximum nutritional value from whole foods so if you're feeding it subpar produce, you're simply not going to reap the full benefits.

That's why it's so important to be discerning when selecting the fruits, vegetables, greens, nuts, seeds and other superfoods that will make up your NutriBullet creations. By taking the time to choose the highest quality, most nutrientdense ingredients available, you'll be setting yourself up for blending success and unlocking an abundance of vital vitamins, minerals, antioxidants and phytonutrients.

Start by focusing on fresh, seasonal produce whenever possible. Locallygrown, inseason fruits and veggies tend to be at the peak of their ripeness and nutrient content, providing you with the most concentrated dose of beneficial plant compounds. And while organic isn't always an option, aim to choose organic varieties whenever you can, as they're typically grown without the use of harmful pesticides and other chemicals that can diminish nutritional value.

Another important consideration is the level of processing. When shopping for items like nuts, seeds, nut butters and the like, look for minimallyprocessed, raw or roastedonly versions that haven't been subjected to extensive heat treatments or the addition of unhealthy oils and fillers. The more intact and unrefined the ingredient, the better it will be for maximizing nutrient absorption.

It's also worth taking a closer look at ingredient labels, especially when it comes to liquids, spices, and any other premade items you might be incorporating into your NutriBullet blends. Steer clear of added sugars, artificial sweeteners, preservatives and other potential inflammatory agents, and instead opt for pure, unadulterated versions. Things like unsweetened nut milks, coldpressed juices, and organic herbs and spices will ensure your blends are as nourishing as possible.

Of course, properly storing your ingredients is just as crucial as the initial selection process. Once you've brought your fresh produce, nuts, seeds and other whole food items home, be sure to keep them properly refrigerated or frozen to maintain their nutritional integrity. This will help prevent spoilage, oxidation and the loss of vital vitamins and minerals.

And when it comes time to actually blend, pay close attention to the order in which you add your ingredients to the NutriBullet. As a general rule, it's best to start with your liquid base first, followed by leafy greens, fruits, nuts, seeds and any other solid elements. This setup ensures the blades have enough liquid to move freely and thoroughly break down even the toughest ingredients.

By keeping these ingredient selection and preparation tips in mind, you'll be well on your way to crafting NutriBullet blends that are not only delicious, but also bursting with concentrated, bioavailable nutrition. After all, what good is a powerful nutrient extraction machine if you're not feeding it the highest quality, most nutrientdense foods nature has to offer? With a little bit of mindful ingredient selection, you can maximize the benefits of your NutriBullet and take your health to new heights.

Nutrient retention through blending techniques

One of the most revolutionary aspects of the NutriBullet is its ability to unlock the maximum nutritional value of the whole food ingredients you blend. Unlike traditional blenders that simply pulverize foods into a rough puree, the NutriBullet's unique extraction process goes a step further, breaking down the cellular walls and releasing a concentrated dose of vitamins, minerals, antioxidants and other beneficial plant compounds.

This remarkable feat is made possible through the NutriBullet's highspeed blending action, which is powered by its exceptional 6001200 watt motor. As the stainless steel blade spins at speeds up to 25,000 RPM, it generates an incredible amount of friction and kinetic energy that thoroughly transforms even the toughest whole food ingredients.

Rather than simply chopping or pureeing, this highvelocity blending action actually ruptures the cell membranes of the fruits, vegetables, greens, nuts and seeds you're blending. This releases all of the vital nutrients that would otherwise remain inaccessible if you were to simply chew and swallow these whole foods.

The end result is a nutrientdense "superfood smoothie" that makes it remarkably easy for your body to rapidly absorb and utilize these vital plantbased compounds. Things like chlorophyll from leafy greens, carotenoids from carrots, flavonoids from berries, and healthy fats from nuts and seeds are all broken down into a liquid form that requires minimal digestive effort.

Compare this to juicing, which extracts only the juice from produce while discarding the nutrientrich fiber. Or even regular blending, which simply turns foods into a chunky puree without fully breaking down the cellular structure. The NutriBullet goes above and beyond, ensuring that you get to reap the complete nutritional bounty of every ingredient you blend.

Of course, properly using your NutriBullet is key to maximizing this nutrient retention. Things like blending order, blending duration, and ingredient selection all play a crucial role. Starting with liquids first, using the tamper tool to guide ingredients toward the blade if needed, and avoiding overblending are all important steps to follow.

It's also vital to steer clear of blending hot ingredients directly in the sealed NutriBullet cups, as the combination of heat and agitation can lead to dangerous pressure buildup. Instead, blend room temperature or chilled items first, then transfer the mixture to a stovetop pot or bowl if you need to heat it through.

By mastering these techniques and best practices, you'll be able to consistently create NutriBullet blends that are not only bursting with delicious flavor, but also jampacked with a rich array of vital nutrients. From immuneboosting vitamin C and bonestrengthening calcium, to guthealing fiber and inflammationfighting antioxidants it's all there, in a portable and easily digestible form.

Ultimately, the ability of the NutriBullet to preserve and concentrate the nutritional integrity of whole foods is what sets it apart from other blenders on the market. By turning the toughest leafy greens, heartiest veggies and most substantial nuts and seeds into a smooth, drinkable elixir, this appliance empowers you to nourish your body with nature's most powerful superfoods like never before. And that's a gamechanging benefit you simply can't afford to overlook on your journey to optimal health and wellness.

CHAPTER 1: SMOOTHIES

Strawberry Banana Smoothie

Prep: 5 mins | Serves: 2

Ingredients:
- US: 1 cup strawberries, hulled | 1 banana, peeled | 1/2 cup plain yogurt | 1/2 cup milk | 1 tablespoon honey | 1 cup ice cubes
- UK: 150g strawberries, hulled | 1 banana, peeled | 120g plain yogurt | 120ml milk | 15ml honey | 120g ice cubes

Instructions:
1. Add strawberries, banana, yogurt, milk, honey, and ice cubes to the Nutribullet cup.
2. Secure the cup onto the Nutribullet base and blend on high speed until smooth, about 30 seconds.
3. Serve immediately and enjoy!

Nutritional Info: Calories: 120 | Fat: 1g | Carbs: 25g | Protein: 3g

Function Used: High Speed Blend

Orange Julius Smoothie

Prep: 5 mins | Serves: 2

Ingredients:
- US: 2 oranges, peeled and segmented | 1/2 cup milk | 1/2 cup orange juice | 1 tablespoon honey | 1 cup ice cubes
- UK: 2 oranges, peeled and segmented | 120ml milk | 120ml orange juice | 15ml honey | 120g ice cubes

Instructions:
1. Place oranges, milk, orange juice, honey, and ice cubes into the Nutribullet cup.
2. Attach the cup to the Nutribullet base and blend on high speed until creamy and smooth, about 45 seconds.
3. Pour into glasses and serve immediately.

Nutritional Info: Calories: 140 | Fat: 1g | Carbs: 30g | Protein: 2g

Function Used: High Speed Blend

Very Berry Smoothie

Prep: 5 mins | Serves: 2

Ingredients:
- US: 1/2 cup strawberries | 1/2 cup blueberries | 1/2 cup raspberries | 1/2 cup blackberries | 1/2 cup plain yogurt | 1/2 cup milk | 1 tablespoon honey | 1 cup ice cubes
- UK: 120g strawberries | 120g blueberries | 120g raspberries | 120g blackberries | 120g plain yogurt | 120ml milk | 15ml honey | 120g ice cubes

Instructions:
1. Add strawberries, blueberries, raspberries, blackberries, yogurt, milk, honey, and ice cubes to the Nutribullet cup.
2. Secure the cup onto the Nutribullet base and blend on high speed until well combined and smooth, about 45 seconds.
3. Pour into glasses and serve immediately.

Nutritional Info: Calories: 150 | Fat: 1g | Carbs: 30g | Protein: 3g

Function Used: High Speed Blend

Peaches and Cream Smoothie

Prep: 5 mins | Serves: 2

Ingredients:
- US: 1 cup sliced peaches | 1/2 cup plain yogurt | 1/2 cup milk | 1 tablespoon honey | 1/4 teaspoon vanilla extract | 1 cup ice cubes
- UK: 150g sliced peaches | 120g plain yogurt | 120ml milk | 15ml honey | 1/4 teaspoon vanilla extract | 120g ice cubes

Instructions:
1. Place sliced peaches, yogurt, milk, honey, vanilla extract, and ice cubes into the Nutribullet cup.
2. Attach the cup to the Nutribullet base and blend on high speed until smooth and creamy, about 45 seconds.
3. Pour into glasses and serve immediately.

Nutritional Info: Calories: 140 | Fat: 1g | Carbs: 30g | Protein: 3g

Function Used: High Speed Blend

Chocolate Peanut Butter Smoothie

Prep: 5 mins | Serves: 2

Ingredients:
- US: 2 tablespoons cocoa powder | 2 tablespoons peanut butter | 1 banana, peeled | 1 cup milk | 1 tablespoon honey | 1 cup ice cubes
- UK: 30g cocoa powder | 30g peanut butter | 1 banana, peeled | 240ml milk | 15ml honey | 120g ice cubes

Instructions:
1. Add cocoa powder, peanut butter, banana, milk, honey, and ice cubes to the Nutribullet cup.
2. Secure the cup onto the Nutribullet base and blend on high speed until creamy and well combined, about 45 seconds.
3. Pour into glasses and serve immediately.

Nutritional Info: Calories: 260 | Fat: 9g | Carbs: 35g | Protein: 10g

Function Used: High Speed Blend

Green Smoothie

Prep: 5 mins | Serves: 2

Ingredients:
- US: 2 cups spinach | 1/2 cup cucumber, sliced | 1/2 avocado, pitted and peeled | 1/2 banana, peeled | 1/2 cup pineapple chunks | 1 cup coconut water | 1 cup ice cubes
- UK: 60g spinach | 60g cucumber, sliced | 1/2 avocado, pitted and peeled | 1/2 banana, peeled | 120g pineapple chunks | 240ml coconut water | 120g ice cubes

Instructions:
- Place spinach, cucumber, avocado, banana, pineapple chunks, coconut water, and ice cubes into the Nutribullet cup.
- Attach the cup to the Nutribullet base and blend on high speed until smooth and creamy, about 45 seconds.
- Pour into glasses and serve immediately.

Nutritional Info: Calories: 180 | Fat: 8g | Carbs: 25g | Protein: 5g

Function Used: High Speed Blend

Tropical Smoothie

Prep: 5 mins | Serves: 2

Ingredients:
- US: 1/2 cup pineapple chunks | 1/2 cup mango chunks | 1/2 banana, peeled | 1/2 cup orange juice | 1/2 cup coconut milk | 1 cup ice cubes
- UK: 120g pineapple chunks | 120g mango chunks | 1/2 banana, peeled | 120ml orange juice | 120ml coconut milk | 120g ice cubes

Instructions:
1. Combine pineapple chunks, mango chunks, banana, orange juice, coconut milk, and ice cubes in the Nutribullet cup.
2. Secure the cup onto the Nutribullet base and blend on high speed until smooth and creamy, about 45 seconds.
3. Pour into glasses and serve immediately.

Nutritional Info: Calories: 200 | Fat: 6g | Carbs: 35g | Protein: 3g

Function Used: High Speed Blend

Blueberry Almond Smoothie

Prep: 5 mins | Serves: 2

Ingredients:
- US: 1 cup blueberries | 1 banana, peeled | 1/4 cup almonds | 1/2 cup Greek yogurt | 1/2 cup almond milk | 1 tablespoon honey | 1 cup ice cubes
- UK: 150g blueberries | 1 banana, peeled | 30g almonds | 120g Greek yogurt | 120ml almond milk | 15ml honey | 120g ice cubes

Instructions:
1. Add blueberries, banana, almonds, Greek yogurt, almond milk, honey, and ice cubes to the Nutribullet cup.
2. Attach the cup to the Nutribullet base and blend on high speed until smooth and creamy, about 45 seconds.
3. Pour into glasses and serve immediately.

Nutritional Info: Calories: 280 | Fat: 11g | Carbs: 35g | Protein: 9g

Function Used: High Speed Blend

Peach Mango Smoothie

Prep: 5 mins | Serves: 2

Ingredients:
- US: 1 cup mango chunks | 1 cup peach slices | 1/2 cup orange juice | 1/2 cup Greek yogurt | 1 tablespoon honey | 1 cup ice cubes
- UK: 150g mango chunks | 150g peach slices | 120ml orange juice | 120g Greek yogurt | 15ml honey | 120g ice cubes

Instructions:
1. Combine mango chunks, peach slices, orange juice, Greek yogurt, honey, and ice cubes in the Nutribullet cup.
2. Secure the cup onto the Nutribullet base and blend on high speed until smooth and creamy, about 45 seconds.
3. Pour into glasses and serve immediately.

Nutritional Info: Calories: 220 | Fat: 2g | Carbs: 45g | Protein: 9g

Function Used: High Speed Blend

Acai Berry Smoothie

Prep: 5 mins | Serves: 2

Ingredients:
- US: 1 pack frozen acai berry puree | 1/2 cup mixed berries (strawberries, blueberries, raspberries) | 1 banana, peeled | 1/2 cup almond milk | 1 tablespoon honey | 1 cup ice cubes
- UK: 100g frozen acai berry puree | 75g mixed berries (strawberries, blueberries, raspberries) | 1 banana, peeled | 120ml almond milk | 15ml honey | 120g ice cubes

Instructions:
1. Break the frozen acai berry puree pack into chunks and add to the Nutribullet cup along with mixed berries, banana, almond milk, honey, and ice cubes.
2. Attach the cup to the Nutribullet base and blend on high speed until smooth and creamy, about 45 seconds.
3. Pour into glasses and serve immediately.

Nutritional Info: Calories: 220 | Fat: 4g | Carbs: 45g | Protein: 3g

Function Used: High Speed Blend

Pomegranate Smoothie

Prep: 5 mins | Serves: 2

Ingredients:
- US: 1/2 cup pomegranate seeds | 1/2 cup strawberries | 1/2 cup raspberries | 1/2 cup Greek yogurt | 1/2 cup pomegranate juice | 1 cup ice cubes
- UK: 75g pomegranate seeds | 75g strawberries | 75g raspberries | 120g Greek yogurt | 120ml pomegranate juice | 120g ice cubes

1. *Instructions:*
1. Combine pomegranate seeds, strawberries, raspberries, Greek yogurt, pomegranate juice, and ice cubes in the Nutribullet cup.
2. Secure the cup onto the Nutribullet base and blend on high speed until smooth and creamy, about 45 seconds.
3. Pour into glasses and serve immediately.

Nutritional Info: Calories: 180 | Fat: 1g | Carbs: 35g | Protein: 8g

Function Used: High Speed Blend

Watermelon Lime Smoothie

Prep: 5 mins | Serves: 2

Ingredients:
- US: 2 cups seedless watermelon chunks | Juice of 2 limes | 1 tablespoon honey | 1 cup ice cubes
- UK: 300g seedless watermelon chunks | Juice of 2 limes | 15ml honey | 120g ice cubes

Instructions:
1. Add watermelon chunks, lime juice, honey, and ice cubes to the Nutribullet cup.
2. Attach the cup to the Nutribullet base and blend on high speed until smooth and creamy, about 45 seconds.
3. Pour into glasses and serve immediately.

Nutritional Info: Calories: 90 | Fat: 0g | Carbs: 22g | Protein: 1g

Function Used: High Speed Blend

Grapefruit Spinach Smoothie

Prep: 5 mins | Serves: 2

Ingredients:
- US: 1 grapefruit, peeled and segmented | 2 cups spinach leaves | 1 banana, peeled | 1/2 cup Greek yogurt | 1/2 cup orange juice | 1 cup ice cubes
- UK: 1 grapefruit, peeled and segmented | 60g spinach leaves | 1 banana, peeled | 120g Greek yogurt | 120ml orange juice | 120g ice cubes

Instructions:
1. Place grapefruit segments, spinach leaves, banana, Greek yogurt, orange juice, and ice cubes into the Nutribullet cup.
2. Secure the cup onto the Nutribullet base and blend on high speed until smooth and creamy, about 45 seconds.
3. Pour into glasses and serve immediately.

Nutritional Info: Calories: 180 | Fat: 1g | Carbs: 35g | Protein: 7g

Function Used: High Speed Blend

Cherry Vanilla Smoothie

Prep: 5 mins | Serves: 2

Ingredients:
- US: 1 cup frozen cherries | 1/2 cup Greek yogurt | 1/2 teaspoon vanilla extract | 1 tablespoon honey | 1 cup almond milk | 1 cup ice cubes
- UK: 150g frozen cherries | 120g Greek yogurt | 2.5ml vanilla extract | 15ml honey | 240ml almond milk | 120g ice cubes

Instructions:
1. Combine frozen cherries, Greek yogurt, vanilla extract, honey, almond milk, and ice cubes in the Nutribullet cup.
2. Attach the cup to the Nutribullet base and blend on high speed until smooth and creamy, about 45 seconds.
3. Pour into glasses and serve immediately.

Nutritional Info: Calories: 180 | Fat: 2g | Carbs: 30g | Protein: 7g

Function Used: High Speed Blend

Pineapple Coconut Smoothie

Prep: 5 mins | Serves: 2

Ingredients:
- US: 1 cup pineapple chunks | 1/2 cup coconut milk | 1/2 cup Greek yogurt | 1/4 cup shredded coconut | 1 tablespoon honey | 1 cup ice cubes
- UK: 150g pineapple chunks | 120ml coconut milk | 120g Greek yogurt | 30g shredded coconut | 15ml honey | 120g ice cubes

Instructions:
1. Add pineapple chunks, coconut milk, Greek yogurt, shredded coconut, honey, and ice cubes to the Nutribullet cup.
2. Secure the cup onto the Nutribullet base and blend on high speed until smooth and creamy, about 45 seconds.
3. Pour into glasses, garnish with additional shredded coconut if desired, and serve immediately.

Nutritional Info: Calories: 220 | Fat: 10g | Carbs: 30g | Protein: 5g

Function Used: High Speed Blend

CHAPTER 2: BREAKFASTS

Nutribullet Pancakes

Prep: 10 mins | Cook: 10 mins | Serves: 4 pancakes

Ingredients:
- US: 1 cup allpurpose flour, 1 tbsp sugar, 2 tsp baking powder, 1/4 tsp salt, 1 egg, 3/4 cup milk, 2 tbsp melted butter
- UK: 120g plain flour, 1 tbsp sugar, 2 tsp baking powder, 1/4 tsp salt, 1 egg, 175ml milk, 30g melted butter

Instructions:
1. Combine flour, sugar, baking powder, and salt in the Nutribullet blender.
2. Add egg, milk, and melted butter.
3. Blend until smooth.
4. Heat a nonstick pan over medium heat and pour batter to form pancakes.
5. Cook until bubbles form on the surface, then flip and cook until golden brown.

Nutritional info: Calories: 150 | Fat: 6g | Carbs: 20g | Protein: 4g

Functions used: Blend

Breakfast Power Bowl

Prep: 15 mins | Cook: 0 mins | Serves: 2 bowls

Ingredients:
- US: 1 banana, 1 cup mixed berries, 1/2 cup Greek yogurt, 1/4 cup granola, 2 tbsp honey
- UK: 1 banana, 150g mixed berries, 120g Greek yogurt, 30g granola, 30ml honey

Instructions:
1. Blend banana, mixed berries, and Greek yogurt until smooth.
2. Divide the mixture into bowls.
3. Top with granola and drizzle with honey.

Nutritional info: Calories: 250 | Fat: 3g | Carbs: 47g | Protein: 9g

Functions used: Blend

Banana Oatmeal Smoothie Bowl

Prep: 5 mins | Cook: 0 mins | Serves: 1 bowl

Ingredients:
- US: 1 banana, 1/2 cup rolled oats, 1/2 cup milk, 1 tbsp honey, 1/4 tsp cinnamon, 1 tbsp peanut butter, 1 tbsp chia seeds (optional)
- UK: 1 banana, 50g rolled oats, 120ml milk, 15ml honey, 1/4 tsp cinnamon, 15g peanut butter, 15g chia seeds (optional)

Instructions:
1. Blend banana, rolled oats, milk, honey, cinnamon, peanut butter, and chia seeds until smooth.
2. Pour into a bowl and top with sliced banana, oats, and a drizzle of honey.

Nutritional info: Calories: 350 | Fat: 10g | Carbs: 55g | Protein: 13g

Functions used: Blend

Peach Parfait Smoothie Bowl

Prep: 10 mins | Cook: 0 mins | Serves: 1 bowl

Ingredients:
- US: 1 ripe peach, 1/2 cup Greek yogurt, 1/4 cup granola, 1 tbsp honey, 1/4 tsp vanilla extract
- UK: 1 ripe peach, 120g Greek yogurt, 30g granola, 15ml honey, 1/4 tsp vanilla extract

Instructions:
1. Blend the ripe peach, Greek yogurt, honey, and vanilla extract until smooth.
2. Pour the mixture into a bowl.
3. Top with granola and sliced peach.

Nutritional info: Calories: 300 | Fat: 3g | Carbs: 60g | Protein: 10g

Functions used: Blend

Berry Yogurt Bowl

Prep: 5 mins | Cook: 0 mins | Serves: 1 bowl

Ingredients:
- US: 1/2 cup mixed berries (strawberries, blueberries, raspberries), 1/2 cup Greek yogurt, 2 tbsp granola, 1 tbsp honey
- UK: 75g mixed berries (strawberries, blueberries, raspberries), 120g Greek yogurt, 30g granola, 15ml honey

Instructions:
1. Layer Greek yogurt and mixed berries in a bowl.
2. Sprinkle granola over the top.
3. Drizzle with honey.

Nutritional info: Calories: 220 | Fat: 3g | Carbs: 35g | Protein: 15g

Functions used: None

Pumpkin Pie Oatmeal

Prep: 5 mins | Cook: 10 mins | Serves: 2 bowls

Ingredients:
- US: 1 cup rolled oats, 1 cup milk, 1/2 cup pumpkin puree, 2 tbsp maple syrup, 1/2 tsp pumpkin pie spice, 1/4 cup chopped pecans
- UK: 100g rolled oats, 240ml milk, 120g pumpkin puree, 30ml maple syrup, 2.5ml pumpkin pie spice, 30g chopped pecans

Instructions:
1. In a saucepan, combine rolled oats and milk. Cook over medium heat until oats are tender.
2. Stir in pumpkin puree, maple syrup, and pumpkin pie spice.
3. Cook for another 23 minutes until heated through.
4. Serve hot, topped with chopped pecans.

Nutritional info: Calories: 320 | Fat: 12g | Carbs: 45g | Protein: 10g

Functions used: Cook

Blueberry Muffin Smoothie Bowl

Prep: 5 mins | Cook: 0 mins | Serves: 1 bowl

Ingredients:
- US: 1/2 cup blueberries, 1/2 banana, 1/2 cup almond milk, 1/4 cup rolled oats, 1 tbsp almond butter, 1 tsp honey
- UK: 75g blueberries, 1/2 banana, 120ml almond milk, 30g rolled oats, 15g almond butter, 5ml honey

Instructions:
1. Combine blueberries, banana, almond milk, rolled oats, almond butter, and honey in the Nutribullet cup.
2. Blend until smooth.
3. Pour into a bowl.
4. Top with additional blueberries, sliced banana, and a sprinkle of rolled oats if desired.

Nutritional info: Calories: 350 | Fat: 12g | Carbs: 55g | Protein: 8g

Functions used: Blend

Frittata in a Mug

Prep: 5 mins | Cook: 3 mins | Serves: 1 mug

Ingredients:
- US: 2 eggs, 2 tbsp milk, 1/4 cup chopped vegetables (bell peppers, spinach, tomatoes), 2 tbsp shredded cheese, salt and pepper to taste
- UK: 2 eggs, 30ml milk, 30g chopped vegetables (bell peppers, spinach, tomatoes), 30g shredded cheese, salt and pepper to taste

Instructions:
1. Crack eggs into a microwavesafe mug.
2. Add milk, chopped vegetables, shredded cheese, salt, and pepper.
3. Whisk until well combined.
4. Microwave on high for 23 minutes or until set.
5. Let it cool for a minute before serving.

Nutritional info: Calories: 280 | Fat: 18g | Carbs: 7g | Protein: 20g

Functions used: None

Spinach and Tomato Scramble

Prep: 5 mins | Cook: 5 mins | Serves: 1

Ingredients:
- US: 2 eggs, 1/4 cup chopped spinach, 1/4 cup diced tomatoes, 1 tbsp olive oil, salt and pepper to taste
- UK: 2 eggs, 30g chopped spinach, 30g diced tomatoes, 15ml olive oil, salt and pepper to taste

Instructions:
1. Heat olive oil in a nonstick skillet over medium heat.
2. Add chopped spinach and diced tomatoes. Cook until spinach is wilted and tomatoes are softened.
3. Crack eggs into the skillet.
4. Scramble until eggs are fully cooked.
5. Season with salt and pepper.

Nutritional info: Calories: 230 | Fat: 16g | Carbs: 5g | Protein: 14g

Functions used: Cook

Tropical Fruit Salad

Prep: 10 mins | Cook: 0 mins | Serves: 2

Ingredients:
- US: 1 cup pineapple chunks, 1 cup mango chunks, 1 cup papaya chunks, 1/2 cup shredded coconut, 1 lime (juiced)
- UK: 150g pineapple chunks, 150g mango chunks, 150g papaya chunks, 50g shredded coconut, 1 lime (juiced)

Instructions:
1. Combine pineapple, mango, papaya, and shredded coconut in a mixing bowl.
2. Squeeze lime juice over the fruit.
3. Toss gently to coat.
4. Serve immediately or refrigerate for later.

Nutritional info: Calories: 220 | Fat: 8g | Carbs: 38g | Protein: 2g

Functions used: None

Overnight Chia Oats

Prep: 5 mins | Cook: 0 mins | Serves: 1

Ingredients:
- US: 1/4 cup rolled oats, 1/2 cup almond milk, 1 tbsp chia seeds, 1/2 tsp vanilla extract, 1 tbsp maple syrup, toppings (fresh fruit, nuts, seeds)
- UK: 30g rolled oats, 120ml almond milk, 15g chia seeds, 2.5ml vanilla extract, 15ml maple syrup, toppings (fresh fruit, nuts, seeds)

Instructions:
1. In a Nutribullet cup, combine rolled oats, almond milk, chia seeds, vanilla extract, and maple syrup.
2. Screw on the extractor blade and blend until smooth.
3. Pour the mixture into a jar or container with a lid.
4. Refrigerate overnight.
5. In the morning, top with fresh fruit, nuts, and seeds before serving.

Nutritional info: Calories: 290 | Fat: 9g | Carbs: 46g | Protein: 7g

Functions used: Blend

Nutribullet Omelet

Prep: 5 mins | Cook: 5 mins | Serves: 1

Ingredients:
- US: 2 eggs, 2 tbsp milk, 1/4 cup chopped vegetables (bell peppers, onions, mushrooms), 1/4 cup shredded cheese, salt and pepper to taste
- UK: 2 eggs, 30ml milk, 30g chopped vegetables (bell peppers, onions, mushrooms), 30g shredded cheese, salt and pepper to taste

Instructions:
1. Crack eggs into a Nutribullet cup.
2. Add milk, chopped vegetables, shredded cheese, salt, and pepper.
3. Screw on the extractor blade and blend until well combined.
4. Pour the mixture into a greased skillet over medium heat.
5. Cook for 34 minutes until the edges start to set.
6. Flip and cook for an additional 12 minutes until fully cooked.
7. Serve hot with toast or a side salad.

Nutritional info: Calories: 320 | Fat: 22g | Carbs: 6g | Protein: 24g

Functions used: Blend, Cook

Breakfast Burrito Bowl

Prep: 10 mins | Cook: 10 mins | Serves: 2

Ingredients:
- US: 4 large eggs, 1/4 cup diced bell peppers, 1/4 cup diced onions, 1/4 cup diced tomatoes, 1/4 cup cooked black beans, 1/4 cup shredded cheddar cheese, 2 tablespoons chopped cilantro, salt and pepper to taste, 1 avocado (sliced), salsa and sour cream for serving
- UK: 4 large eggs, 30g diced bell peppers, 30g diced onions, 30g diced tomatoes, 30g cooked black beans, 30g shredded cheddar cheese, 2 tablespoons chopped cilantro, salt and pepper to taste, 1 avocado (sliced), salsa and sour cream for serving

Instructions:
1. In a Nutribullet cup, blend the eggs until smooth.
2. Heat a skillet over medium heat and add a splash of oil.
3. Pour the blended eggs into the skillet and cook until they start to set.
4. Add the diced bell peppers, onions, tomatoes, and black beans to the skillet.
5. Stir gently and cook until the vegetables are tender and the eggs are fully cooked.
6. Season with salt and pepper to taste.

7. Divide the mixture into two bowls.
8. Top each bowl with shredded cheddar cheese, chopped cilantro, sliced avocado, salsa, and sour cream.
9. Serve hot and enjoy!

Nutritional info: Calories: 390 | Fat: 27g | Carbs: 18g | Protein: 21g

Functions used: Blend, Cook

Breakfast Quinoa with Berries

Prep: 5 mins | Cook: 15 mins | Serves: 2

Ingredients:
- US: 1/2 cup quinoa, 1 cup almond milk, 1 tablespoon honey, 1/2 teaspoon cinnamon, 1/2 cup mixed berries (strawberries, blueberries, raspberries), 2 tablespoons chopped nuts (walnuts, almonds), additional honey for drizzling
- UK: 100g quinoa, 240ml almond milk, 15ml honey, 2.5ml cinnamon, 75g mixed berries (strawberries, blueberries, raspberries), 30g chopped nuts (walnuts, almonds), additional honey for drizzling

Instructions:
1. Rinse the quinoa under cold water using a finemesh sieve.
2. In a saucepan, combine quinoa, almond milk, honey, and cinnamon.
3. Bring to a boil, then reduce the heat to low and simmer for 15 minutes, or until the quinoa is tender and the liquid is absorbed.
4. Fluff the quinoa with a fork and divide it into two bowls.
5. Top each bowl with mixed berries and chopped nuts.
6. Drizzle with additional honey if desired.
7. Serve warm and enjoy!

Nutritional info: Calories: 320 | Fat: 10g | Carbs: 52g | Protein: 8g

Functions used: None

CHAPTER 3: APPETIZERS AND SNACKS

Nutribullet Hummus

Prep: 10 mins | Cook: 0 mins | Serves: 6

Ingredients:
- US: 1 can (15 oz) chickpeas, drained and rinsed, 1/4 cup tahini, 1/4 cup olive oil, 1/4 cup lemon juice, 2 cloves garlic, minced, 1/2 teaspoon cumin, salt and pepper to taste, 23 tablespoons water (optional, for consistency)
- UK: 1 can (400g) chickpeas, drained and rinsed, 60g tahini, 60ml olive oil, 60ml lemon juice, 2 cloves garlic, minced, 1/2 teaspoon cumin, salt and pepper to taste, 3045ml water (optional, for consistency)

Instructions:
1. Add chickpeas, tahini, olive oil, lemon juice, minced garlic, cumin, salt, and pepper to the Nutribullet cup.
2. Blend on high speed until smooth and creamy, adding water as needed to reach desired consistency.
3. Taste and adjust seasoning if necessary.
4. Transfer hummus to a serving bowl and drizzle with a little extra olive oil.
5. Serve with pita bread, crackers, or vegetable sticks.

Nutritional info: Calories: 180 | Fat: 12g | Carbs: 14g | Protein: 6g

Functions used: Blend

Guacamole

Prep: 10 mins | Cook: 0 mins | Serves: 4

Ingredients:
- US: 2 ripe avocados, 1/4 cup diced onion, 1/4 cup diced tomato, 2 tablespoons chopped cilantro, 1 clove garlic, minced, 1 lime, juiced, salt and pepper to taste
- UK: 2 ripe avocados, 30g diced onion, 30g diced tomato, 2 tablespoons chopped cilantro, 1 clove garlic, minced, 1 lime, juiced, salt and pepper to taste

Instructions:
1. Scoop the flesh of the avocados into the Nutribullet cup.
2. Add diced onion, diced tomato, chopped cilantro, minced garlic, and lime juice.
3. Season with salt and pepper.
4. Blend until smooth or desired consistency is reached.
5. Taste and adjust seasoning if needed.
6. Transfer guacamole to a serving bowl and serve with tortilla chips or vegetable sticks.

Nutritional info: Calories: 120 | Fat: 10g | Carbs: 8g | Protein: 2g

Functions used: Blend

Nutribullet Salsa

Prep: 10 mins | Cook: 0 mins | Serves: 4

Ingredients:
- US: 2 tomatoes, diced, 1/4 cup diced onion, 1/4 cup chopped cilantro, 1 jalapeno pepper, seeded and diced, 1 clove garlic, minced, 1 lime, juiced, salt and pepper to taste
- UK: 2 tomatoes, diced, 30g diced onion, 30g chopped cilantro, 1 jalapeno pepper, seeded and diced, 1 clove garlic, minced, 1 lime, juiced, salt and pepper to taste

Instructions:
1. Add diced tomatoes, diced onion, chopped cilantro, diced jalapeno pepper, minced garlic, and lime juice to the Nutribullet cup.
2. Season with salt and pepper.
3. Blend until desired consistency is reached.
4. Taste and adjust seasoning if necessary.
5. Transfer salsa to a serving bowl and serve with tortilla chips or use as a topping for tacos or salads.

Nutritional info: Calories: 20 | Fat: 0g | Carbs: 5g | Protein: 1g

Functions used: Blend

Kale Pesto

Prep: 10 mins | Cook: 0 mins | Serves: 4

Ingredients:
- US: 2 cups kale leaves, stems removed, 1/4 cup fresh basil leaves, 1/4 cup grated Parmesan cheese, 1/4 cup toasted pine nuts, 1 clove garlic, minced, 1/4 cup olive oil, salt and pepper to taste
- UK: 60g kale leaves, stems removed, 15g fresh basil leaves, 25g grated Parmesan cheese, 25g toasted pine nuts, 1 clove garlic, minced, 60ml olive oil, salt and pepper to taste

Instructions:
1. Place kale leaves, basil leaves, Parmesan cheese, toasted pine nuts, minced garlic, and olive oil into the Nutribullet cup.
2. Season with salt and pepper.
3. Blend until smooth, scraping down the sides as needed.
4. Taste and adjust seasoning if necessary.
5. Transfer pesto to a jar and refrigerate until ready to use.

Nutritional info: Calories: 150 | Fat: 14g | Carbs: 3g | Protein: 4g

Functions used: Blend

Coconut Whipped Cream

Prep: 5 mins | Cook: 0 mins | Serves: 4

Ingredients:
- US: 1 can (13.5 oz) fullfat coconut milk, chilled, 1 tbsp powdered sugar (optional), 1 tsp vanilla extract
- UK: 1 can (400ml) fullfat coconut milk, chilled, 15g powdered sugar (optional), 5ml vanilla extract

Instructions:
1. Scoop the solid coconut cream from the chilled can into the Nutribullet cup, leaving the liquid behind.
2. Add powdered sugar (if using) and vanilla extract.
3. Blend until smooth and creamy.
4. Taste and add more sugar or vanilla if desired.
5. Use immediately as a topping for desserts or refrigerate until ready to use.

Nutritional info: Calories: 120 | Fat: 12g | Carbs: 2g | Protein: 1g

Functions used: Blend

Nut and Seed Trail Mix

Prep: 5 mins | Cook: 0 mins | Serves: 4

Ingredients:
- US: 1/2 cup almonds, 1/2 cup cashews, 1/4 cup pumpkin seeds, 1/4 cup sunflower seeds, 1/4 cup dried cranberries, 1/4 cup dark chocolate chips
- UK: 60g almonds, 60g cashews, 30g pumpkin seeds, 30g sunflower seeds, 30g dried cranberries, 30g dark chocolate chips

Instructions:
1. Add almonds, cashews, pumpkin seeds, sunflower seeds, dried cranberries, and dark chocolate chips to the Nutribullet cup.
2. Pulse a few times until the ingredients are roughly chopped and mixed.
3. Transfer the trail mix to an airtight container for storage.
4. Enjoy as a healthy snack on the go or sprinkle over yogurt or oatmeal.

Nutritional info: Calories: 200 | Fat: 15g | Carbs: 15g | Protein: 5g

Functions used: Pulse

Energy Bites

Prep: 15 mins | Cook: 0 mins | Serves: 12

Ingredients:
- US: 1 cup rolled oats, 1/2 cup peanut butter, 1/4 cup honey, 1/4 cup mini chocolate chips, 1/4 cup chopped nuts, 1 tsp vanilla extract
- UK: 90g rolled oats, 125g peanut butter, 60ml honey, 60ml mini chocolate chips, 30g chopped nuts, 5ml vanilla extract

Instructions:
1. Combine rolled oats, peanut butter, honey, chocolate chips, chopped nuts, and vanilla extract in the Nutribullet cup.
2. Pulse until well combined and the mixture starts to clump together.
3. Scoop out small portions of the mixture and roll into balls using your hands.
4. Place the energy bites on a baking sheet lined with parchment paper.
5. Refrigerate for at least 30 minutes to firm up before serving.

Nutritional info: Calories: 150 | Fat: 8g | Carbs: 17g | Protein: 4g

Functions used: Pulse

Green Goddess Dip

Prep: 10 mins | Cook: 0 mins | Serves: 6

Ingredients:
- US: 1 ripe avocado, 1/2 cup Greek yogurt, 1/4 cup fresh parsley leaves, 1/4 cup fresh basil leaves, 2 tbsp lemon juice, 1 clove garlic, salt and pepper to taste
- UK: 1 ripe avocado, 120g Greek yogurt, 15g fresh parsley leaves, 15g fresh basil leaves, 30ml lemon juice, 1 clove garlic, salt and pepper to taste

Instructions:
1. Scoop the flesh of the avocado into the Nutribullet cup.
2. Add Greek yogurt, parsley leaves, basil leaves, lemon juice, garlic, salt, and pepper.
3. Blend until smooth and creamy.
4. Taste and adjust seasoning if needed.
5. Transfer the dip to a serving bowl and refrigerate until ready to serve.

Nutritional info: Calories: 70 | Fat: 5g | Carbs: 4g | Protein: 3g

Functions used: Blend

Roasted Red Pepper Dip

Prep: 15 mins | Cook: 20 mins | Serves: 6

Ingredients:
- US: 2 large red bell peppers, 1/4 cup Greek yogurt, 2 tbsp olive oil, 2 cloves garlic, 1 tsp lemon juice, 1/2 tsp paprika, salt and pepper to taste
- UK: 2 large red bell peppers, 60g Greek yogurt, 30ml olive oil, 2 cloves garlic, 5ml lemon juice, 2.5ml paprika, salt and pepper to taste

Instructions:
1. Preheat the oven to 425°F (220°C). Place whole red bell peppers on a baking sheet and roast for 20 minutes, turning occasionally, until charred and tender.
2. Remove the peppers from the oven and let cool slightly. Peel off the charred skin, remove seeds and stems, and roughly chop the flesh.
3. Add the roasted red peppers, Greek yogurt, olive oil, garlic, lemon juice, paprika, salt, and pepper to the Nutribullet cup.
4. Blend until smooth and creamy.
5. Taste and adjust seasoning if necessary.
6. Transfer the dip to a serving bowl and refrigerate until ready to serve.

Nutritional info: Calories: 60 | Fat: 4g | Carbs: 5g | Protein: 2g

Functions used: Blend

Spinach and Artichoke Dip

Prep: 15 mins | Cook: 25 mins | Serves: 6

Ingredients:
- US: 1 cup frozen spinach, thawed and drained, 1 cup canned artichoke hearts, drained and chopped, 1/2 cup Greek yogurt, 1/4 cup mayonnaise, 1/4 cup grated Parmesan cheese, 1/4 cup shredded mozzarella cheese, 1 clove garlic, minced, salt and pepper to taste
- UK: 240g frozen spinach, thawed and drained, 240g canned artichoke hearts, drained and chopped, 120g Greek yogurt, 60g mayonnaise, 25g grated Parmesan cheese, 25g shredded mozzarella cheese, 1 clove garlic, minced, salt and pepper to taste

Instructions:
1. Preheat the oven to 375°F (190°C).
2. In a Nutribullet cup, combine the spinach, artichoke hearts, Greek yogurt, mayonnaise, Parmesan cheese, mozzarella cheese, garlic, salt, and pepper.
3. Blend until well combined but still slightly chunky.
4. Transfer the mixture to a baking dish and spread it out evenly.
5. Bake for 25 minutes, or until bubbly and golden brown on top.
6. Serve hot with tortilla chips or crackers.

Nutritional info: Calories: 120 | Fat: 9g | Carbs: 5g | Protein: 7g

Functions used: Blend, Bake

Nutribullet Salad Dressings

Prep: 5 mins | Cook: 0 mins | Serves: 4

Ingredients:
- US: 1/4 cup olive oil, 2 tbsp balsamic vinegar, 1 tsp Dijon mustard, 1 clove garlic, minced, 1/2 tsp honey, salt and pepper to taste
- UK: 60ml olive oil, 30ml balsamic vinegar, 5ml Dijon mustard, 1 clove garlic, minced, 2.5ml honey, salt and pepper to taste

Instructions:
1. Add olive oil, balsamic vinegar, Dijon mustard, minced garlic, honey, salt, and pepper to the Nutribullet cup.
2. Blend until well combined and emulsified.
3. Taste and adjust seasoning if necessary.
4. Transfer the dressing to a jar or bottle and store in the refrigerator until ready to use.
5. Shake well before serving.

Nutritional info: Calories: 90 | Fat: 10g | Carbs: 2g | Protein: 0g

Functions used: Blend

Tzatziki Sauce

Prep: 10 mins | Cook: 0 mins | Serves: 4

Ingredients:
- US: 1 cup Greek yogurt, 1/2 cucumber, peeled and seeded, 2 cloves garlic, minced, 1 tbsp lemon juice, 1 tbsp fresh dill, chopped, salt and pepper to taste
- UK: 240g Greek yogurt, 1/2 cucumber, peeled and seeded, 2 cloves garlic, minced, 15ml lemon juice, 15ml fresh dill, chopped, salt and pepper to taste

Instructions:
1. Grate the cucumber using a grater or a Nutribullet.
2. Squeeze the grated cucumber in a clean kitchen towel to remove excess moisture.
3. In a Nutribullet cup, combine the Greek yogurt, grated cucumber, minced garlic, lemon juice, and chopped dill.
4. Blend until smooth.
5. Season with salt and pepper to taste.
6. Transfer the tzatziki sauce to a serving bowl and refrigerate until ready to serve.

Nutritional info: Calories: 60 | Fat: 0g | Carbs: 6g | Protein: 8g

Functions used: Blend, Grate

Fruit Smoothie Popsicles

Prep: 10 mins | Cook: 4 hours | Serves: 6

Ingredients:
- US: 1 cup mixed berries (strawberries, blueberries, raspberries), 1 banana, 1/2 cup Greek yogurt, 1/2 cup coconut water, 1 tbsp honey (optional)
- UK: 240g mixed berries (strawberries, blueberries, raspberries), 1 banana, 120g Greek yogurt, 120ml coconut water, 15ml honey (optional)

Instructions:
1. In a Nutribullet cup, combine the mixed berries, banana, Greek yogurt, coconut water, and honey (if using).
2. Blend until smooth.
3. Pour the mixture into popsicle molds.
4. Insert popsicle sticks and freeze for at least 4 hours, or until firm.
5. To unmold, run warm water over the outside of the molds for a few seconds and gently pull out the popsicles.

Nutritional info: Calories: 70 | Fat: 0.5g | Carbs: 15g | Protein: 3g

Functions used: Blend, Freeze

Chocolate Banana Popsicles

Prep: 10 mins | Cook: 4 hours | Serves: 6

Ingredients:
- US: 2 ripe bananas, 1/4 cup cocoa powder, 1/2 cup Greek yogurt, 1/2 cup milk (of your choice), 1 tbsp honey (optional)
- UK: 2 ripe bananas, 25g cocoa powder, 120g Greek yogurt, 120ml milk (of your choice), 15ml honey (optional)

Instructions:
1. In a Nutribullet cup, combine the ripe bananas, cocoa powder, Greek yogurt, milk, and honey (if using).
2. Blend until smooth.
3. Pour the mixture into popsicle molds.
4. Insert popsicle sticks and freeze for at least 4 hours, or until firm.
5. To unmold, run warm water over the outside of the molds for a few seconds and gently pull out the popsicles.

Nutritional info: Calories: 90 | Fat: 1g | Carbs: 20g | Protein: 3g

Functions used: Blend, Freeze

CHAPTER 4: SOUPS AND STEWS

Velvety Butternut Squash Soup

Prep: 15 mins | Cook: 25 mins | Serves: 4

Ingredients:
- US: 1 medium butternut squash (about 2 lbs), peeled, seeded, and cubed, 1 onion, chopped, 2 cloves garlic, minced, 4 cups vegetable broth, 1 tsp ground cinnamon, salt and pepper to taste
- UK: 1 medium butternut squash (about 900g), peeled, seeded, and cubed, 1 onion, chopped, 2 cloves garlic, minced, 950ml vegetable broth, 1 tsp ground cinnamon, salt and pepper to taste

Instructions:
1. In a pot, combine the butternut squash, onion, garlic, and vegetable broth.
2. Bring to a boil, then reduce heat and simmer until the squash is tender, about 2025 minutes.
3. Using a ladle, transfer the mixture to the Nutribullet cup. Add ground cinnamon, salt, and pepper.
4. Blend until smooth and creamy.
5. Pour the soup back into the pot and reheat if necessary before serving.

Nutritional info: Calories: 120 | Fat: 0.5g | Carbs: 30g | Protein: 2g

Functions used: Simmer, Blend

Creamy Broccoli Cheddar Soup

Prep: 10 mins | Cook: 20 mins | Serves: 4

Ingredients:
- US: 1 head broccoli, chopped, 1 onion, chopped, 2 cups vegetable broth, 1 cup milk, 1 cup shredded cheddar cheese, salt and pepper to taste
- UK: 1 head broccoli, chopped, 1 onion, chopped, 475ml vegetable broth, 240ml milk, 100g shredded cheddar cheese, salt and pepper to taste

Instructions:
1. In a pot, combine the chopped broccoli, onion, and vegetable broth.
2. Bring to a boil, then reduce heat and simmer until the broccoli is tender, about 1520 minutes.
3. Using a ladle, transfer the mixture to the Nutribullet cup. Add milk, shredded cheddar cheese, salt, and pepper.
4. Blend until smooth and creamy.

5. Pour the soup back into the pot and reheat gently until the cheese is melted.

Nutritional info: Calories: 220 | Fat: 12g | Carbs: 15g | Protein: 14g

Functions used: Simmer, Blend, Melt

Classic Tomato Basil Soup

Prep: 10 mins | Cook: 25 mins | Serves: 4

Ingredients:
- US: 1 can (28 oz) whole tomatoes, 1 onion, chopped, 2 cloves garlic, minced, 2 cups vegetable broth, 1/4 cup fresh basil leaves, salt and pepper to taste
- UK: 1 can (400g) whole tomatoes, 1 onion, chopped, 2 cloves garlic, minced, 475ml vegetable broth, 15g fresh basil leaves, salt and pepper to taste

Instructions:
1. In a pot, combine the canned tomatoes (with juices), chopped onion, garlic, and vegetable broth.
2. Bring to a boil, then reduce heat and simmer for about 20 minutes.
3. Add fresh basil leaves to the pot and stir to combine.
4. Using a ladle, transfer the mixture to the Nutribullet cup.
5. Blend until smooth.
6. Pour the soup back into the pot and reheat if necessary.
7. Season with salt and pepper to taste before serving.

Nutritional info: Calories: 80 | Fat: 0.5g | Carbs: 18g | Protein: 3g

Functions used: Simmer, Blend

Comforting Carrot Ginger Soup

Prep: 15 mins | Cook: 25 mins | Serves: 4

Ingredients:
- US: 4 large carrots, peeled and chopped, 1 onion, chopped, 2 cloves garlic, minced, 2inch piece fresh ginger, peeled and grated, 4 cups vegetable broth, salt and pepper to taste, coconut milk for garnish (optional)
- UK: 4 large carrots, peeled and chopped, 1 onion, chopped, 2 cloves garlic, minced, 5cm piece fresh ginger, peeled and grated, 950ml vegetable broth, salt and pepper to taste, coconut milk for garnish (optional)

Instructions:
1. In a pot, combine the chopped carrots, onion, garlic, grated ginger, and vegetable broth.

2. Bring to a boil, then reduce heat and simmer until the carrots are tender, about 20-25 minutes.
3. Using a ladle, transfer the mixture to the Nutribullet cup.
4. Blend until smooth.
5. Pour the soup back into the pot and reheat if necessary.
6. Season with salt and pepper to taste.
7. Serve hot, garnished with a swirl of coconut milk if desired.

Nutritional info: Calories: 120 | Fat: 1g | Carbs: 26g | Protein: 3g

Functions used: Simmer, Blend

Creamy Potato Leek Soup

Prep: 15 mins | Cook: 30 mins | Serves: 4

Ingredients:
- US: 3 large potatoes, peeled and diced, 2 leeks, white and light green parts chopped, 2 cloves garlic, minced, 4 cups vegetable broth, 1/2 cup heavy cream, salt and pepper to taste, chopped chives for garnish
- UK: 3 large potatoes, peeled and diced, 2 leeks, white and light green parts chopped, 2 cloves garlic, minced, 950ml vegetable broth, 120ml double cream, salt and pepper to taste, chopped chives for garnish

Instructions:
1. In a pot, combine the diced potatoes, chopped leeks, minced garlic, and vegetable broth.
2. Bring to a boil, then reduce heat and simmer until the potatoes are tender, about 20-25 minutes.
3. Using a ladle, transfer the mixture to the Nutribullet cup.
4. Blend until smooth.
5. Pour the blended soup back into the pot.
6. Stir in the heavy cream and heat gently until warmed through.
7. Season with salt and pepper to taste.
8. Serve hot, garnished with chopped chives.

Nutritional info: Calories: 280 | Fat: 12g | Carbs: 38g | Protein: 5g

Functions used: Simmer, Blend

Roasted Cauliflower Soup

Prep: 10 mins | Cook: 35 mins | Serves: 4

Ingredients:
- US: 1 head cauliflower, cut into florets, 1 onion, chopped, 2 cloves garlic, minced, 4 cups vegetable broth, 1/4 cup olive oil, salt and pepper to taste, fresh thyme leaves for garnish
- UK: 1 head cauliflower, cut into florets, 1 onion, chopped, 2 cloves garlic, minced, 950ml vegetable broth, 60ml olive oil, salt and pepper to taste, fresh thyme leaves for garnish

Instructions:
1. Preheat the oven to 400°F (200°C).
2. On a baking sheet, toss the cauliflower florets, chopped onion, and minced garlic with olive oil, salt, and pepper.
3. Roast in the preheated oven for about 2530 minutes until the cauliflower is golden brown.
4. Transfer the roasted vegetables to a pot, add vegetable broth, and bring to a simmer.
5. Simmer for 5 minutes, then remove from heat.
6. Using a ladle, transfer the mixture to the Nutribullet cup.
7. Blend until smooth.
8. Pour the blended soup back into the pot and reheat if necessary.
9. Season with salt and pepper to taste.
10. Serve hot, garnished with fresh thyme leaves.

Nutritional info: Calories: 180 | Fat: 14g | Carbs: 14g | Protein: 4g

Functions used: Roast, Simmer, Blend

Lentil Stew

Prep: 15 mins | Cook: 40 mins | Serves: 6

Ingredients:
- US: 1 cup dried lentils, 1 onion, diced, 2 carrots, diced, 2 celery stalks, diced, 2 cloves garlic, minced, 4 cups vegetable broth, 1 can (14 oz) diced tomatoes, 1 teaspoon ground cumin, 1 teaspoon paprika, salt and pepper to taste, fresh parsley for garnish
- UK: 200g dried lentils, 1 onion, diced, 2 carrots, diced, 2 celery stalks, diced, 2 cloves garlic, minced, 950ml vegetable broth, 1 can (400g) diced tomatoes, 1 teaspoon ground cumin, 1 teaspoon paprika, salt and pepper to taste, fresh parsley for garnish

Instructions:
1. In a pot, combine the dried lentils, diced onion, carrots, celery, minced garlic, vegetable broth, diced tomatoes, ground cumin, and paprika.

2. Bring to a boil, then reduce heat and simmer, covered, for 30-35 minutes until the lentils and vegetables are tender.
3. Using a ladle, transfer half of the stew mixture to the Nutribullet cup.
4. Blend until smooth.
5. Pour the blended mixture back into the pot and stir to combine.
6. Season with salt and pepper to taste.
7. Serve hot, garnished with fresh parsley.

Nutritional info: Calories: 180 | Fat: 1g | Carbs: 32g | Protein: 12g

Functions used: Simmer, Blend

Minestrone Soup

Prep: 15 mins | Cook: 30 mins | Serves: 6

Ingredients:
- US: 2 tablespoons olive oil, 1 onion, diced, 2 carrots, diced, 2 celery stalks, diced, 2 cloves garlic, minced, 4 cups vegetable broth, 1 can (14 oz) diced tomatoes, 1 can (15 oz) kidney beans, drained and rinsed, 1 cup small pasta, 2 cups chopped spinach, 1 teaspoon dried oregano, 1 teaspoon dried basil, salt and pepper to taste, grated Parmesan cheese for serving
- UK: 30ml olive oil, 1 onion, diced, 2 carrots, diced, 2 celery stalks, diced, 2 cloves garlic, minced, 950ml vegetable broth, 1 can (400g) diced tomatoes, 1 can (400g) kidney beans, drained and rinsed, 180g small pasta, 200g chopped spinach, 1 teaspoon dried oregano, 1 teaspoon dried basil, salt and pepper to taste, grated Parmesan cheese for serving

Instructions:
1. In a pot, heat the olive oil over medium heat.
2. Add the diced onion, carrots, celery, and minced garlic. Cook until vegetables are tender, about 5-7 minutes.
3. Add the vegetable broth, diced tomatoes, kidney beans, small pasta, dried oregano, and dried basil.
4. Bring to a boil, then reduce heat and simmer for 15-20 minutes until the pasta is cooked.
5. Stir in the chopped spinach and cook for an additional 2-3 minutes until wilted.
6. Season with salt and pepper to taste.
7. Serve hot, garnished with grated Parmesan cheese.

Nutritional info: Calories: 280 | Fat: 4g | Carbs: 48g | Protein: 14g

Functions used: Simmer

Thai Coconut Curry Soup

Prep: 15 mins | Cook: 25 mins | Serves: 4

Ingredients:
- US: 1 tablespoon coconut oil, 1 onion, diced, 2 cloves garlic, minced, 1 tablespoon fresh ginger, grated, 2 tablespoons Thai red curry paste, 4 cups vegetable broth, 1 can (14 oz) coconut milk, 2 cups diced sweet potato, 1 cup sliced mushrooms, 1 cup chopped kale, 1 tablespoon soy sauce, 1 tablespoon lime juice, salt and pepper to taste, fresh cilantro for garnish
- UK: 15ml coconut oil, 1 onion, diced, 2 cloves garlic, minced, 1 tablespoon fresh ginger, grated, 30g Thai red curry paste, 950ml vegetable broth, 1 can (400ml) coconut milk, 400g diced sweet potato, 200g sliced mushrooms, 200g chopped kale, 15ml soy sauce, 15ml lime juice, salt and pepper to taste, fresh cilantro for garnish

Instructions:
- In a pot, heat the coconut oil over medium heat.
- Add the diced onion, minced garlic, and grated ginger. Cook until fragrant, about 23 minutes.
- Stir in the Thai red curry paste and cook for another 12 minutes.
- Add the vegetable broth, coconut milk, diced sweet potato, and sliced mushrooms. Bring to a simmer and cook for 1520 minutes until the sweet potatoes are tender.
- Stir in the chopped kale, soy sauce, and lime juice. Cook for an additional 23 minutes until the kale is wilted.
- Season with salt and pepper to taste.
- Serve hot, garnished with fresh cilantro.

Nutritional info: Calories: 320 | Fat: 23g | Carbs: 27g | Protein: 5g

Functions used: Simmer

Black Bean Soup

Prep: 10 mins | Cook: 25 mins | Serves: 4

Ingredients:
- US: 1 tablespoon olive oil, 1 onion, diced, 2 cloves garlic, minced, 2 cans (15 oz each) black beans, drained and rinsed, 4 cups vegetable broth, 1 can (14 oz) diced tomatoes, 1 teaspoon ground cumin, 1 teaspoon chili powder, 1/2 teaspoon smoked paprika, salt and pepper to taste, fresh cilantro for garnish
- UK: 15ml olive oil, 1 onion, diced, 2 cloves garlic, minced, 2 cans (400g each) black beans, drained and rinsed, 950ml vegetable broth, 1 can (400g) diced tomatoes, 5g ground cumin, 5g chili powder, 2.5g smoked paprika, salt and pepper to taste, fresh cilantro for garnish

Instructions:
1. In a pot, heat the olive oil over medium heat.
2. Add the diced onion and minced garlic. Cook until softened, about 34 minutes.
3. Add one can of black beans to the pot. Using the Nutribullet, blend the remaining can of black beans with a cup of vegetable broth until smooth.
4. Pour the blended black bean mixture into the pot along with the whole black beans.
5. Stir in the diced tomatoes, ground cumin, chili powder, and smoked paprika.
6. Bring to a simmer and cook for 1520 minutes, stirring occasionally.
7. Season with salt and pepper to taste.
8. Serve hot, garnished with fresh cilantro.

Nutritional info: Calories: 240 | Fat: 4g | Carbs: 40g | Protein: 12g

Functions used: Blend, Simmer

Creamy Mushroom Soup

Prep: 15 mins | Cook: 25 mins | Serves: 4

Ingredients:
- US: 2 tablespoons unsalted butter, 1 onion, diced, 2 cloves garlic, minced, 16 oz cremini mushrooms, sliced, 4 cups vegetable broth, 1/2 cup heavy cream, 2 tablespoons allpurpose flour, salt and pepper to taste, fresh thyme leaves for garnish
- UK: 30g unsalted butter, 1 onion, diced, 2 cloves garlic, minced, 450g cremini mushrooms, sliced, 950ml vegetable broth, 120ml double cream, 30g allpurpose flour, salt and pepper to taste, fresh thyme leaves for garnish

Instructions:
1. In a pot, melt the butter over medium heat.
2. Add the diced onion and minced garlic. Cook until softened, about 34 minutes.
3. Add the sliced mushrooms to the pot. Cook until they release their moisture and start to brown, about 57 minutes.
4. Sprinkle the flour over the mushrooms and stir to coat.
5. Slowly pour in the vegetable broth while stirring continuously to prevent lumps from forming.
6. Bring the mixture to a simmer and cook for 1015 minutes until slightly thickened.
7. Stir in the heavy cream and cook for another 5 minutes.
8. Season with salt and pepper to taste.
9. Serve hot, garnished with fresh thyme leaves.

Nutritional info: Calories: 220 | Fat: 16g | Carbs: 15g | Protein: 6g

Functions used: Simmer

Italian Wedding Soup

Prep: 20 mins | Cook: 30 mins | Serves: 6

Ingredients:
- US: 1 tablespoon olive oil, 1 onion, diced, 2 carrots, diced, 2 stalks celery, diced, 2 cloves garlic, minced, 6 cups chicken broth, 8 oz small pasta (such as orzo or acini di pepe), 1 lb Italian sausage, 4 cups spinach, chopped, salt and pepper to taste, grated Parmesan cheese for garnish
- UK: 15ml olive oil, 1 onion, diced, 2 carrots, diced, 2 stalks celery, diced, 2 cloves garlic, minced, 1.4 litres chicken broth, 225g small pasta (such as orzo or acini di pepe), 450g Italian sausage, 200g spinach, chopped, salt and pepper to taste, grated Parmesan cheese for garnish

Instructions:
1. In a pot, heat the olive oil over medium heat.
2. Add the diced onion, carrots, celery, and minced garlic. Cook until softened, about 57 minutes.
3. Pour in the chicken broth and bring to a simmer.
4. Add the pasta to the pot and cook according to package instructions until al dente.
5. Meanwhile, form the Italian sausage into small meatballs and cook in a separate skillet until browned and cooked through.
6. Once the pasta is cooked, stir in the cooked meatballs and chopped spinach.
7. Simmer for another 5 minutes until the spinach is wilted.
8. Season with salt and pepper to taste.
9. Serve hot, garnished with grated Parmesan cheese.

Nutritional info: Calories: 380 | Fat: 20g | Carbs: 30g | Protein: 20g

Functions used: Simmer

Chicken Noodle Soup

Prep: 15 mins | Cook: 25 mins | Serves: 4

Ingredients:
- US: 1 tablespoon olive oil, 1 onion, diced, 2 carrots, sliced, 2 stalks celery, sliced, 2 cloves garlic, minced, 6 cups chicken broth, 8 oz egg noodles, 2 cups shredded cooked chicken, salt and pepper to taste, fresh parsley for garnish
- UK: 15ml olive oil, 1 onion, diced, 2 carrots, sliced, 2 stalks celery, sliced, 2 cloves garlic, minced, 1.4 litres chicken broth, 225g egg noodles, 450g shredded cooked chicken, salt and pepper to taste, fresh parsley for garnish

Instructions:
1. Heat olive oil in a large pot over medium heat.
2. Add diced onion, sliced carrots, sliced celery, and minced garlic. Cook until softened, about 5-7 minutes.
3. Pour in chicken broth and bring to a boil.
4. Add egg noodles to the pot and cook according to package instructions until tender.
5. Stir in shredded cooked chicken and simmer for another 5 minutes to heat through.
6. Season with salt and pepper to taste.
7. Serve hot, garnished with fresh parsley.

Nutritional info: Calories: 320 | Fat: 10g | Carbs: 30g | Protein: 25g

Functions used: Boil, Simmer

Roasted Red Pepper Soup

Prep: 15 mins | Cook: 35 mins | Serves: 4

Ingredients:
- US: 4 red bell peppers, halved and seeded, 1 onion, chopped, 2 cloves garlic, minced, 2 tablespoons olive oil, 4 cups vegetable broth, 1 can (14 oz) diced tomatoes, drained, 1 teaspoon smoked paprika, salt and pepper to taste, fresh basil for garnish
- UK: 4 red bell peppers, halved and seeded, 1 onion, chopped, 2 cloves garlic, minced, 30ml olive oil, 950ml vegetable broth, 1 can (400g) diced tomatoes, drained, 5g smoked paprika, salt and pepper to taste, fresh basil for garnish

Instructions:
1. Preheat the oven to 400°F (200°C).
2. Place the red bell pepper halves on a baking sheet, cut side down. Roast in the oven for 20-25 minutes until charred and softened.
3. In a large pot, heat olive oil over medium heat. Add chopped onion and minced garlic. Cook until translucent, about 5 minutes.
4. Add the roasted red peppers to the pot along with vegetable broth, diced tomatoes, and smoked paprika. Bring to a simmer.
5. Simmer for 10 minutes, then remove from heat.
6. Use a Nutribullet to blend the soup until smooth.
7. Season with salt and pepper to taste.
8. Serve hot, garnished with fresh basil.

Nutritional info: Calories: 180 | Fat: 7g | Carbs: 25g | Protein: 4g

Functions used: Roast, Simmer, Blend

CHAPTER 5: SAUCES AND SPREADS

Simple Tomato Sauce

Prep: 10 mins | Cook: 20 mins | Serves: 4

Ingredients:
- US: 1 can (28 oz) crushed tomatoes, 2 cloves garlic, minced, 2 tablespoons olive oil, 1 teaspoon dried oregano, 1 teaspoon dried basil, salt and pepper to taste
- UK: 1 can (800g) crushed tomatoes, 2 cloves garlic, minced, 30ml olive oil, 5g dried oregano, 5g dried basil, salt and pepper to taste

Instructions:
1. In a saucepan, heat olive oil over medium heat.
2. Add minced garlic and sauté until fragrant, about 1 minute.
3. Pour in crushed tomatoes and stir in dried oregano and basil.
4. Simmer the sauce for 15-20 minutes, stirring occasionally, until thickened.
5. Season with salt and pepper to taste.
6. Use a Nutribullet to blend the sauce until smooth, if desired.

Nutritional info: Calories: 80 | Fat: 5g | Carbs: 8g | Protein: 2g

Functions used: Sauté, Simmer, Blend

Alfredo Sauce

Prep: 5 mins | Cook: 10 mins | Serves: 4

Ingredients:
- US: 1 cup heavy cream, 1/2 cup grated Parmesan cheese, 2 cloves garlic, minced, 2 tablespoons butter, salt and pepper to taste, chopped parsley for garnish
- UK: 240ml double cream, 50g grated Parmesan cheese, 2 cloves garlic, minced, 30g butter, salt and pepper to taste, chopped parsley for garnish

Instructions:
1. In a saucepan, melt butter over medium heat.
2. Add minced garlic and sauté for 1-2 minutes until fragrant.
3. Pour in heavy cream and bring to a simmer.
4. Stir in grated Parmesan cheese until melted and smooth.
5. Season with salt and pepper to taste.
6. Simmer the sauce for 5-7 minutes until thickened.
7. Garnish with chopped parsley before serving.

Nutritional info: Calories: 250 | Fat: 23g | Carbs: 3g | Protein: 6g

Functions used: Sauté, Simmer

Basil Pesto

Prep: 10 mins | Serves: 6

Ingredients:
- US: 2 cups fresh basil leaves, 1/2 cup grated Parmesan cheese, 1/2 cup pine nuts, 2 cloves garlic, 1/4 cup olive oil, salt and pepper to taste
- UK: 50g fresh basil leaves, 50g grated Parmesan cheese, 50g pine nuts, 2 cloves garlic, 60ml olive oil, salt and pepper to taste

Instructions:
1. In a Nutribullet cup, combine basil leaves, Parmesan cheese, pine nuts, garlic, and olive oil.
2. Blend until smooth, scraping down the sides as needed.
3. Season with salt and pepper to taste.
4. Store in an airtight container in the refrigerator for up to 1 week.

Nutritional info: Calories: 180 | Fat: 18g | Carbs: 2g | Protein: 4g

Functions used: Blend

Cilantro Lime Crema

Prep: 5 mins | Serves: 4

Ingredients:
- US: 1 cup Greek yogurt, 1/4 cup chopped cilantro, juice of 1 lime, 1 clove garlic, minced, salt and pepper to taste
- UK: 240ml Greek yogurt, 15g chopped cilantro, juice of 1 lime, 1 clove garlic, minced, salt and pepper to taste

Instructions:
1. In a Nutribullet cup, combine Greek yogurt, chopped cilantro, lime juice, and minced garlic.
2. Blend until smooth and creamy.
3. Season with salt and pepper to taste.
4. Serve as a topping for tacos, salads, or grilled meats.

Nutritional info: Calories: 60 | Fat: 0g | Carbs: 6g | Protein: 9g

Functions used: Blend

BBQ Sauce

Prep: 5 mins | Cook: 10 mins | Serves: 6

Ingredients:
- US: 1 cup ketchup, 1/4 cup brown sugar, 2 tablespoons apple cider vinegar, 1 tablespoon Worcestershire sauce, 1 teaspoon smoked paprika, 1/2 teaspoon garlic powder, 1/2 teaspoon onion powder, salt and pepper to taste
- UK: 240ml ketchup, 50g brown sugar, 30ml apple cider vinegar, 15ml Worcestershire sauce, 5g smoked paprika, 2g garlic powder, 2g onion powder, salt and pepper to taste

Instructions:
1. In a saucepan, combine all ingredients over medium heat.
2. Bring the mixture to a simmer, then reduce heat to low.
3. Simmer the sauce for 5-10 minutes, stirring occasionally, until thickened.
4. Let cool before using as a marinade or dipping sauce.

Nutritional info: Calories: 70 | Fat: 0g | Carbs: 18g | Protein: 0g

Functions used: Simmer

Tahini Sauce

Prep: 5 mins | Serves: 6

Ingredients:
- US: 1/2 cup tahini, 1/4 cup water, 2 tablespoons lemon juice, 1 clove garlic, minced, 1/2 teaspoon salt
- UK: 120g tahini, 60ml water, 30ml lemon juice, 1 clove garlic, minced, 1/2 teaspoon salt

Instructions:
1. In a Nutribullet cup, combine tahini, water, lemon juice, minced garlic, and salt.
2. Blend until smooth and creamy, adding more water if necessary to reach desired consistency.
3. Adjust seasoning to taste, adding more salt or lemon juice if needed.
4. Serve as a dip for vegetables or drizzle over roasted vegetables or falafel.

Nutritional info: Calories: 100 | Fat: 9g | Carbs: 4g | Protein: 3g

Functions used: Blend

Olive Tapenade

Prep: 10 mins | Serves: 8

Ingredients:
- US: 1 cup pitted Kalamata olives, 1/4 cup chopped parsley, 2 tablespoons capers, 1 clove garlic, minced, 2 tablespoons lemon juice, 2 tablespoons olive oil
- UK: 150g pitted Kalamata olives, 15g chopped parsley, 30ml capers, 1 clove garlic, minced, 30ml lemon juice, 30ml olive oil

Instructions:
1. In a Nutribullet cup, combine Kalamata olives, chopped parsley, capers, minced garlic, lemon juice, and olive oil.
2. Pulse until the ingredients are coarsely chopped and well combined.
3. Adjust seasoning to taste, adding more lemon juice or olive oil if desired.
4. Transfer to a serving dish and serve with crusty bread or crackers.

Nutritional info: Calories: 50 | Fat: 5g | Carbs: 1g | Protein: 0g

Functions used: Pulse

Sundried Tomato Spread

Prep: 10 mins | Serves: 6

Ingredients:
- US: 1 cup sundried tomatoes (packed in oil), drained, 1/4 cup pine nuts, 2 cloves garlic, minced, 1/4 cup grated Parmesan cheese, 2 tablespoons olive oil, salt and pepper to taste
- UK: 150g sundried tomatoes (packed in oil), drained, 30g pine nuts, 2 cloves garlic, minced, 30g grated Parmesan cheese, 30ml olive oil, salt and pepper to taste

Instructions:
1. In a Nutribullet cup, combine sundried tomatoes, pine nuts, minced garlic, Parmesan cheese, and olive oil.
2. Blend until smooth, scraping down the sides as needed.
3. Season with salt and pepper to taste.
4. Serve as a spread on sandwiches or as a dip for crackers or vegetable sticks.

Nutritional info: Calories: 130 | Fat: 10g | Carbs: 8g | Protein: 4g

Functions used: Blend

Marinara Sauce

Prep: 15 mins | Cook: 20 mins | Serves: 4

Ingredients:
- US: 1 can (14 oz) diced tomatoes, 2 cloves garlic, minced, 1 tablespoon olive oil, 1 teaspoon dried oregano, 1 teaspoon dried basil, salt and pepper to taste
- UK: 400g can diced tomatoes, 2 cloves garlic, minced, 15ml olive oil, 5g dried oregano, 5g dried basil, salt and pepper to taste

Instructions:
1. In a saucepan, heat olive oil over medium heat. Add minced garlic and sauté until fragrant, about 1 minute.
2. Add diced tomatoes (with their juices), dried oregano, and dried basil. Season with salt and pepper to taste.
3. Simmer the sauce over low heat for 1520 minutes, stirring occasionally, until it thickens slightly.
4. Once cooked, transfer the sauce to a Nutribullet cup and blend until smooth.
5. Adjust seasoning if needed and serve over cooked pasta or use as a pizza sauce.

Nutritional info: Calories: 60 | Fat: 4g | Carbs: 6g | Protein: 2g

Functions used: Blend

Peanut Sauce

Prep: 10 mins | Serves: 6

Ingredients:
- US: 1/2 cup peanut butter, 1/4 cup soy sauce, 2 tablespoons rice vinegar, 1 tablespoon honey or maple syrup, 1 clove garlic, minced, 1 teaspoon grated ginger, water as needed
- UK: 120g peanut butter, 60ml soy sauce, 30ml rice vinegar, 15ml honey or maple syrup, 1 clove garlic, minced, 5g grated ginger, water as needed

Instructions:
1. In a Nutribullet cup, combine peanut butter, soy sauce, rice vinegar, honey or maple syrup, minced garlic, and grated ginger.
2. Blend until smooth, adding water as needed to reach the desired consistency.
3. Taste and adjust the flavor by adding more soy sauce for saltiness or honey for sweetness.
4. Serve as a dipping sauce for spring rolls, satay skewers, or drizzle over cooked noodles or stirfried vegetables.

Nutritional info: Calories: 150 | Fat: 12g | Carbs: 7g | Protein: 6g

Functions used: Blend

Mango Chutney

Prep: 15 mins | Cook: 20 mins | Serves: 8

Ingredients:
- US: 2 ripe mangoes, peeled and diced, 1/2 cup white vinegar, 1/4 cup brown sugar, 1/4 cup raisins, 1/4 cup chopped onion, 1 clove garlic, minced, 1 teaspoon grated ginger, 1/4 teaspoon ground cinnamon, 1/4 teaspoon ground cloves, salt to taste
- UK: 2 ripe mangoes, peeled and diced, 120ml white vinegar, 60g brown sugar, 30g raisins, 30g chopped onion, 1 clove garlic, minced, 5g grated ginger, 1/4 teaspoon ground cinnamon, 1/4 teaspoon ground cloves, salt to taste

Instructions:
1. In a saucepan, combine diced mangoes, white vinegar, brown sugar, raisins, chopped onion, minced garlic, grated ginger, ground cinnamon, and ground cloves.
2. Bring the mixture to a simmer over medium heat, then reduce the heat to low and cook for 1520 minutes, stirring occasionally, until the chutney thickens.
3. Season with salt to taste and let cool slightly.
4. Transfer the mixture to a Nutribullet cup and blend until smooth or leave it chunky if desired.
5. Allow the chutney to cool completely before serving. Store in an airtight container in the refrigerator.

Nutritional info: Calories: 80 | Fat: 0.5g | Carbs: 20g | Protein: 1g

Functions used: Blend

Coconut Curry Sauce

Prep: 10 mins | Cook: 15 mins | Serves: 4

Ingredients:
- US: 1 can (13.5 oz) coconut milk, 2 tablespoons red curry paste, 1 tablespoon soy sauce, 1 tablespoon maple syrup or brown sugar, 1 tablespoon lime juice, 1 teaspoon grated ginger, 2 cloves garlic, minced
- UK: 400ml can coconut milk, 30g red curry paste, 15ml soy sauce, 15ml maple syrup or brown sugar, 15ml lime juice, 5g grated ginger, 2 cloves garlic, minced

Instructions:
1. In a saucepan, combine coconut milk, red curry paste, soy sauce, maple syrup or brown sugar, lime juice, grated ginger, and minced garlic.
2. Cook over medium heat, stirring constantly, until the sauce begins to simmer.

3. Reduce the heat to low and let the sauce simmer gently for about 10-15 minutes, allowing the flavors to meld.
4. Once the sauce is done, transfer it to a Nutribullet cup and blend until smooth and creamy.
5. Taste and adjust the seasoning if needed, adding more soy sauce for saltiness or lime juice for acidity.

Nutritional info: Calories: 250 | Fat: 23g | Carbs: 9g | Protein: 3g

Functions used: Blend

Cranberry Sauce

Prep: 5 mins | Cook: 10 mins | Serves: 6

Ingredients:
- US: 1 bag (12 oz) fresh or frozen cranberries, 1 cup granulated sugar, 1/2 cup orange juice, 1 teaspoon orange zest
- UK: 340g bag fresh or frozen cranberries, 200g granulated sugar, 120ml orange juice, 5g orange zest

Instructions:
1. In a saucepan, combine cranberries, granulated sugar, orange juice, and orange zest.
2. Bring the mixture to a boil over medium heat, then reduce the heat to low and let it simmer for about 10 minutes, stirring occasionally, until the cranberries burst and the sauce thickens.
3. Remove from heat and let the sauce cool slightly.
4. Transfer the mixture to a Nutribullet cup and blend until smooth.
5. Allow the cranberry sauce to cool completely before serving. Store in the refrigerator.

Nutritional info: Calories: 120 | Fat: 0g | Carbs: 31g | Protein: 0g

Functions used: Blend

Maple Dijon Vinaigrette

Prep: 5 mins | Serves: 4

Ingredients:
- US: 1/4 cup olive oil, 2 tablespoons apple cider vinegar, 1 tablespoon Dijon mustard, 1 tablespoon maple syrup, salt and pepper to taste
- UK: 60ml olive oil, 30ml apple cider vinegar, 15ml Dijon mustard, 15ml maple syrup, salt and pepper to taste

Instructions:

1. In a Nutribullet cup, combine olive oil, apple cider vinegar, Dijon mustard, maple syrup, salt, and pepper.
2. Blend until well combined and emulsified.
3. Taste and adjust the seasoning if needed, adding more salt, pepper, or maple syrup according to your preference.
4. Serve the vinaigrette over salads or use it as a marinade for grilled vegetables or meats.

Nutritional info: Calories: 120 | Fat: 14g | Carbs: 2g | Protein: 0g

Functions used: Blend

CHAPTER 6: NUT AND SEED BUTTERS

Almond Butter

Prep: 10 mins | Cook: N/A | Serves: About 1 cup

Ingredients:
- US: 2 cups almonds
- UK: 280g almonds

Instructions:
- Add the almonds to your Nutribullet cup.
- Secure the extractor blade onto the cup.
- Blend on high speed for about 5-7 minutes or until creamy, scraping down the sides as needed.
- Store the almond butter in an airtight container in the refrigerator.

Nutritional info: Calories: 180 | Fat: 16g | Carbs: 6g | Protein: 7g

Functions used: Blend

Cashew Butter

Prep: 10 mins | Cook: N/A | Serves: About 1 cup

Ingredients:
- US: 2 cups cashews
- UK: 280g cashews

Instructions:
1. Place the cashews in the Nutribullet cup.
2. Attach the extractor blade and blend on high speed for 5-7 minutes until smooth, scraping down the sides as needed.
3. Transfer the cashew butter to a clean jar and store it in the refrigerator.

Nutritional info: Calories: 160 | Fat: 12g | Carbs: 9g | Protein: 5g

Functions used: Blend

Sunflower Seed Butter

Prep: 10 mins | Cook: N/A | Serves: About 1 cup

Ingredients:
- US: 1 1/2 cups sunflower seeds
- UK: 210g sunflower seeds

Instructions:
1. Add the sunflower seeds to the Nutribullet cup.
2. Secure the extractor blade and blend on high speed for 57 minutes until smooth, scraping down the sides as needed.
3. Transfer the sunflower seed butter to a jar and store it in the refrigerator.

Nutritional info: Calories: 170 | Fat: 14g | Carbs: 7g | Protein: 7g

Functions used: Blend

Chocolate Hazelnut Butter

Prep: 10 mins | Cook: N/A | Serves: About 1 cup

Ingredients:
- US: 1 cup hazelnuts, 1/4 cup cocoa powder, 23 tbsp maple syrup, pinch of salt
- UK: 140g hazelnuts, 30g cocoa powder, 3045ml maple syrup, pinch of salt

Instructions:
1. Toast the hazelnuts in a preheated oven at 350°F (180°C) for 810 minutes, until fragrant and lightly golden.
2. Let the hazelnuts cool slightly, then transfer them to the Nutribullet cup.
3. Add cocoa powder, maple syrup, and a pinch of salt.
4. Secure the extractor blade and blend on high speed for 57 minutes, scraping down the sides as needed, until smooth and creamy.
5. Transfer the chocolate hazelnut butter to a jar and store it in the refrigerator.

Nutritional info: Calories: 180 | Fat: 14g | Carbs: 12g | Protein: 4g

Functions used: Blend

Cookie Dough Almond Butter

Prep: 10 mins | Cook: N/A | Serves: About 1 cup

Ingredients:
- US: 1 cup almonds, 2 tbsp maple syrup, 1/2 tsp vanilla extract, 1/4 cup chocolate chips
- UK: 140g almonds, 30ml maple syrup, 2.5ml vanilla extract, 45g chocolate chips

Instructions:
1. Add the almonds, maple syrup, and vanilla extract to the Nutribullet cup.
2. Secure the extractor blade and blend on high speed for 57 minutes until smooth, scraping down the sides as needed.
3. Stir in the chocolate chips.
4. Transfer the cookie dough almond butter to a jar and store it in the refrigerator.

Nutritional info: Calories: 190 | Fat: 15g | Carbs: 11g | Protein: 6g

Functions used: Blend

Strawberry Almond Butter

Prep: 10 mins | Cook: N/A | Serves: About 1 cup

Ingredients:
- US: 1 cup almonds, 1 cup fresh strawberries, 2 tbsp honey
- UK: 140g almonds, 140g fresh strawberries, 30ml honey

Instructions:
1. Place the almonds in the Nutribullet cup.
2. Add fresh strawberries and honey.
3. Secure the extractor blade and blend on high speed for 57 minutes until smooth, scraping down the sides as needed.
4. Transfer the strawberry almond butter to a jar and store it in the refrigerator.

Nutritional info: Calories: 220 | Fat: 18g | Carbs: 13g | Protein: 7g

Functions used: Blend

Pumpkin Seed Butter

Prep: 10 mins | Cook: N/A | Serves: About 1 cup

Ingredients:
- US: 1 cup pumpkin seeds, 2 tbsp honey or maple syrup, 1/2 tsp cinnamon, pinch of salt
- UK: 140g pumpkin seeds, 30ml honey or maple syrup, 2.5ml cinnamon, pinch of salt

Instructions:
1. Toast the pumpkin seeds in a dry skillet over medium heat for 57 minutes, stirring frequently, until golden and fragrant.
2. Transfer the toasted pumpkin seeds to the Nutribullet cup.
3. Add honey or maple syrup, cinnamon, and a pinch of salt.
4. Secure the extractor blade and blend on high speed for 57 minutes until smooth, scraping down the sides as needed.
5. Transfer the pumpkin seed butter to a jar and store it in the refrigerator.

Nutritional info: Calories: 180 | Fat: 14g | Carbs: 9g | Protein: 7g

Functions used: Blend

Cinnamon Walnut Butter

Prep: 10 mins | Cook: N/A | Serves: About 1 cup

Ingredients:
- US: 1 cup walnuts, 2 tbsp honey, 1 tsp ground cinnamon, pinch of salt
- UK: 140g walnuts, 30ml honey, 5ml ground cinnamon, pinch of salt

Instructions:
1. Place the walnuts in the Nutribullet cup.
2. Add honey, ground cinnamon, and a pinch of salt.
3. Secure the extractor blade and blend on high speed for 57 minutes until smooth, scraping down the sides as needed.
4. Transfer the cinnamon walnut butter to a jar and store it in the refrigerator.

Nutritional info: Calories: 210 | Fat: 20g | Carbs: 7g | Protein: 5g

Functions used: Blend

Maple Pecan Butter

Prep: 10 mins | Cook: N/A | Serves: About 1 cup

Ingredients:
- US: 1 cup pecans, 2 tbsp maple syrup, 1/4 tsp vanilla extract, pinch of salt
- UK: 140g pecans, 30ml maple syrup, 1.25ml vanilla extract, pinch of salt

Instructions:
1. Place the pecans in the Nutribullet cup.
2. Add maple syrup, vanilla extract, and a pinch of salt.
3. Secure the extractor blade and blend on high speed for 57 minutes until smooth, scraping down the sides as needed.
4. Transfer the maple pecan butter to a jar and store it in the refrigerator.

Nutritional info: Calories: 220 | Fat: 22g | Carbs: 7g | Protein: 3g

Functions used: Blend

Coconut Butter

Prep: 10 mins | Cook: N/A | Serves: About 1 cup

Ingredients:
- US: 2 cups unsweetened shredded coconut
- UK: 160g unsweetened shredded coconut

Instructions:
1. Add the shredded coconut to the Nutribullet cup.
2. Secure the extractor blade and blend on high speed for 57 minutes until smooth, scraping down the sides as needed.
3. If the coconut butter is too thick, you can add a teaspoon of coconut oil to help it blend more smoothly.
4. Transfer the coconut butter to a jar and store it in the refrigerator.

Nutritional info: Calories: 280 | Fat: 27g | Carbs: 11g | Protein: 2g

Functions used: Blend

Peanut Butter

Prep: 10 mins | Cook: N/A | Serves: About 1 cup

Ingredients:
- US: 2 cups roasted peanuts, 12 tbsp honey (optional), pinch of salt
- UK: 280g roasted peanuts, 1530ml honey (optional), pinch of salt

Instructions:
1. Add the roasted peanuts to the Nutribullet cup.
2. If desired, add honey and a pinch of salt for flavor.
3. Secure the extractor blade and blend on high speed for 57 minutes until smooth, scraping down the sides as needed.
4. Taste and adjust sweetness or saltiness if necessary.
5. Transfer the peanut butter to a jar and store it in the refrigerator.

Nutritional info: Calories: 180 | Fat: 15g | Carbs: 6g | Protein: 8g

Functions used: Blend

Tahini

Prep: 10 mins | Cook: N/A | Serves: About 1 cup

Ingredients:
- US: 1 cup sesame seeds, 23 tbsp olive oil
- UK: 140g sesame seeds, 3045ml olive oil

Instructions:
1. Toast the sesame seeds in a dry skillet over medium heat for 57 minutes, stirring frequently, until golden brown and fragrant.
2. Let the sesame seeds cool slightly, then transfer them to the Nutribullet cup.
3. Add olive oil to the sesame seeds.

4. Secure the extractor blade and blend on high speed for 57 minutes until smooth, scraping down the sides as needed.
5. If the tahini is too thick, you can add more olive oil until you reach your desired consistency.
6. Transfer the tahini to a jar and store it in the refrigerator.

Nutritional info: Calories: 130 | Fat: 12g | Carbs: 4g | Protein: 5g

Functions used: Blend

Chai Spiced Walnut Butter

Prep: 10 mins | Cook: N/A | Serves: About 1 cup

Ingredients:
- US: 2 cups walnuts, 2 tsp chai spice mix (cinnamon, cardamom, ginger, cloves, nutmeg)
- UK: 280g walnuts, 10ml chai spice mix (cinnamon, cardamom, ginger, cloves, nutmeg)

Instructions:
1. Add the walnuts and chai spice mix to the Nutribullet cup.
2. Secure the extractor blade and blend on high speed for 57 minutes until smooth, scraping down the sides as needed.
3. Taste and adjust the amount of chai spice mix if desired.
4. Transfer the chai spiced walnut butter to a jar and store it in the refrigerator.

Nutritional info: Calories: 180 | Fat: 18g | Carbs: 4g | Protein: 4g

Functions used: Blend

Chocolate Almond Butter

Prep: 10 mins | Cook: N/A | Serves: About 1 cup

Ingredients:
- US: 2 cups almonds, 23 tbsp cocoa powder, 23 tbsp honey (optional)
- UK: 280g almonds, 3045ml cocoa powder, 3045ml honey (optional)

Instructions:
1. Add the almonds, cocoa powder, and honey (if using) to the Nutribullet cup.
2. Secure the extractor blade and blend on high speed for 57 minutes until smooth, scraping down the sides as needed.
3. Taste and adjust sweetness or cocoa flavor if necessary.
4. Transfer the chocolate almond butter to a jar and store it in the refrigerator.

Nutritional info: Calories: 200 | Fat: 16g | Carbs: 9g | Protein: 7g

Functions used: Blend

CHAPTER 7: DESSERTS

Almond Butter Bites

Prep: 15 mins | Cook: 0 mins | Serves: 12 bites

Ingredients:
- US: 1 cup almond butter, 1/4 cup honey, 1 cup rolled oats, 1/4 cup chocolate chips
- UK: 240g almond butter, 60ml honey, 100g rolled oats, 60g chocolate chips

Instructions:
1. Combine almond butter, honey, and rolled oats in a bowl.
2. Roll the mixture into small bitesized balls.
3. Place chocolate chips in the Nutribullet cup and pulse until chopped.
4. Roll the almond butter bites in the chopped chocolate chips.
5. Chill in the refrigerator for 30 minutes before serving.

Nutritional info: Calories: 150 | Fat: 9g | Carbs: 15g | Protein: 4g

Functions used: Pulse

Chocolate Avocado Mousse

Prep: 10 mins | Cook: 0 mins | Serves: 2

Ingredients:
- US: 1 ripe avocado, 1/4 cup cocoa powder, 1/4 cup honey, 1/2 tsp vanilla extract
- UK: 1 ripe avocado, 30g cocoa powder, 60ml honey, 2.5ml vanilla extract

Instructions:
1. Scoop out the avocado flesh into the Nutribullet cup.
2. Add cocoa powder, honey, and vanilla extract.
3. Blend until smooth and creamy.
4. Divide into serving glasses and chill for at least 1 hour before serving.

Nutritional info: Calories: 230 | Fat: 15g | Carbs: 26g | Protein: 4g

Functions used: Blend

Coconut Macaroons

Prep: 10 mins | Cook: 15 mins | Serves: 12 macaroons

Ingredients:
- US: 2 cups shredded coconut, 1/2 cup condensed milk, 1 tsp vanilla extract, 2 egg whites
- UK: 160g shredded coconut, 120ml condensed milk, 5ml vanilla extract, 2 egg whites

Instructions:
1. Preheat oven to 325°F (160°C) and line a baking sheet with parchment paper.
2. In a bowl, mix shredded coconut, condensed milk, and vanilla extract.
3. In the Nutribullet cup, whisk egg whites until stiff peaks form.
4. Gently fold egg whites into the coconut mixture.
5. Drop spoonfuls of the mixture onto the prepared baking sheet.
6. Bake for 15 minutes or until lightly golden.

Nutritional info: Calories: 130 | Fat: 7g | Carbs: 14g | Protein: 2g

Functions used: Blend, Whisk

Chocolate Banana Protein Muffins

Prep: 15 mins | Cook: 20 mins | Serves: 12 muffins

Ingredients:
- US: 2 ripe bananas, 2 eggs, 1/4 cup honey, 1/4 cup coconut oil, 1 cup almond flour, 1/4 cup cocoa powder, 1 scoop chocolate protein powder, 1 tsp baking powder
- UK: 2 ripe bananas, 2 eggs, 60ml honey, 60ml coconut oil, 120g almond flour, 30g cocoa powder, 1 scoop chocolate protein powder, 5ml baking powder

Instructions:
1. Preheat oven to 350°F (180°C) and line a muffin tin with paper liners.
2. In the Nutribullet cup, blend bananas, eggs, honey, and coconut oil until smooth.
3. Add almond flour, cocoa powder, protein powder, and baking powder to the cup and blend until well combined.
4. Pour the batter into the prepared muffin tin, filling each cup 3/4 full.
5. Bake for 1820 minutes or until a toothpick inserted into the center comes out clean.

Nutritional info: Calories: 150 | Fat: 8g | Carbs: 15g | Protein: 5g

Functions used: Blend

Black Bean Brownies

Prep: 10 mins | Cook: 25 mins | Serves: 16 brownies

Ingredients:
- US: 1 can black beans (drained and rinsed), 2 large eggs, 1/4 cup cocoa powder, 2/3 cup honey, 1/4 cup coconut oil, 1/2 tsp baking powder, 1/4 cup chocolate chips (optional)
- UK: 1 can black beans (drained and rinsed), 2 large eggs, 30g cocoa powder, 160ml honey, 60ml coconut oil, 2.5ml baking powder, 40g chocolate chips (optional)

Instructions:
1. Preheat oven to 350°F (180°C) and grease a baking pan.
2. In the Nutribullet cup, blend black beans, eggs, cocoa powder, honey, coconut oil, and baking powder until smooth.
3. Fold in chocolate chips if using.
4. Pour the batter into the prepared baking pan and spread evenly.
5. Bake for 25-30 minutes or until the edges are set.

Nutritional info: Calories: 120 | Fat: 5g | Carbs: 17g | Protein: 3g

Functions used: Blend

Mango Sorbet

Prep: 5 mins | Cook: 0 mins | Serves: 2

Ingredients:
- US: 2 cups frozen mango chunks, 1/4 cup coconut water, 1 tbsp honey (optional), 1/2 lime (juiced)
- UK: 320g frozen mango chunks, 60ml coconut water, 15ml honey (optional), 1/2 lime (juiced)

Instructions:
1. Add frozen mango chunks, coconut water, honey (if using), and lime juice to the Nutribullet cup.
2. Blend until smooth and creamy.
3. Serve immediately as a soft serve or freeze for 1-2 hours for a firmer texture.

Nutritional info: Calories: 120 | Fat: 1g | Carbs: 31g | Protein: 2g

Functions used: Blend

Banana "Ice Cream"

Prep: 5 mins | Cook: 0 mins | Serves: 2

Ingredients:
- US: 2 ripe bananas, sliced and frozen
- UK: 2 ripe bananas, sliced and frozen

Instructions:
1. Place the frozen banana slices into the Nutribullet cup.
2. Blend on high until smooth and creamy, scraping down the sides as needed.
3. Serve immediately as softserve or freeze for 30 minutes for a firmer texture.

Nutritional info: Calories: 105 | Fat: 0.4g | Carbs: 27g | Protein: 1.3g

Functions used: Blend

Pumpkin Pie Smoothie

Prep: 5 mins | Cook: 0 mins | Serves: 1

Ingredients:
- US: 1/2 cup canned pumpkin puree, 1/2 frozen banana, 1/2 cup almond milk, 1/4 tsp pumpkin pie spice, 1 tbsp maple syrup (optional), handful of ice
- UK: 120g canned pumpkin puree, 1/2 frozen banana, 120ml almond milk, 1/4 tsp pumpkin pie spice, 15ml maple syrup (optional), handful of ice

Instructions:
1. Add all ingredients to the Nutribullet cup.
2. Blend until smooth and creamy.
3. Taste and adjust sweetness if needed by adding more maple syrup.
4. Pour into a glass and sprinkle with additional pumpkin pie spice if desired.

Nutritional info: Calories: 160 | Fat: 1g | Carbs: 39g | Protein: 3g

Functions used: Blend

Strawberry Sorbet

Prep: 5 mins | Cook: 0 mins | Serves: 2

Ingredients:
- US: 2 cups frozen strawberries, 2 tbsp honey (optional), 1/4 cup coconut water
- UK: 320g frozen strawberries, 30ml honey (optional), 60ml coconut water

Instructions:
1. Place the frozen strawberries, honey (if using), and coconut water into the Nutribullet cup.
2. Blend until smooth and creamy.
3. Serve immediately as a soft serve or freeze for 12 hours for a firmer texture.

Nutritional info: Calories: 100 | Fat: 0.3g | Carbs: 25g | Protein: 1g

Functions used: Blend

Peanut Butter Banana "Ice Cream"

Prep: 5 mins | Cook: 0 mins | Serves: 2

Ingredients:
- US: 2 ripe bananas, sliced and frozen, 2 tbsp peanut butter
- UK: 2 ripe bananas, sliced and frozen, 30g peanut butter

Instructions:
1. Place the frozen banana slices and peanut butter into the Nutribullet cup.
2. Blend on high until smooth and creamy, scraping down the sides as needed.
3. Serve immediately for a softserve consistency or freeze for 30 minutes for a firmer texture.

Nutritional info: Calories: 195 | Fat: 7g | Carbs: 32g | Protein: 4g

Functions used: Blend

Chia Seed Pudding

Prep: 5 mins | Cook: 4 hours | Serves: 2

Ingredients:
- US: 1/4 cup chia seeds, 1 cup almond milk, 1 tbsp maple syrup (optional), 1/2 tsp vanilla extract
- UK: 40g chia seeds, 240ml almond milk, 15ml maple syrup (optional), 2.5ml vanilla extract

Instructions:
1. In a Nutribullet cup, combine the chia seeds, almond milk, maple syrup (if using), and vanilla extract.

2. Blend on low speed for a few seconds until well mixed.
3. Refrigerate for at least 4 hours or overnight, stirring occasionally, until thickened.
4. Serve chilled with your favorite toppings, such as fresh fruit or nuts.

Nutritional info: Calories: 140 | Fat: 7g | Carbs: 16g | Protein: 5g

Functions used: Blend

Blueberry Crumble

Prep: 10 mins | Cook: 30 mins | Serves: 4

Ingredients:
- US: 2 cups fresh or frozen blueberries, 1/4 cup rolled oats, 1/4 cup almond flour, 2 tbsp maple syrup, 1 tbsp coconut oil, pinch of cinnamon
- UK: 320g fresh or frozen blueberries, 30g rolled oats, 30g almond flour, 30ml maple syrup, 15ml coconut oil, pinch of cinnamon

Instructions:
1. Preheat the oven to 350°F (175°C).
2. In a Nutribullet cup, combine the blueberries and maple syrup. Blend until slightly chunky.
3. In a separate bowl, mix the rolled oats, almond flour, coconut oil, and cinnamon until crumbly.
4. Pour the blueberry mixture into a baking dish and sprinkle the oat mixture evenly on top.
5. Bake for 2530 minutes, or until the topping is golden brown and the blueberries are bubbling.
6. Serve warm with a dollop of yogurt or ice cream, if desired.

Nutritional info: Calories: 150 | Fat: 6g | Carbs: 24g | Protein: 2g

Functions used: Blend, Bake

Dark Chocolate Bark

Prep: 10 mins | Cook: 1 hour | Serves: 6

Ingredients:
- US: 8 oz dark chocolate, chopped, 1/4 cup almonds, chopped, 1/4 cup dried cranberries, 1/4 tsp sea salt
- UK: 225g dark chocolate, chopped, 30g almonds, chopped, 30g dried cranberries, 1/4 tsp sea salt

Instructions:
1. Melt the dark chocolate in a microwavesafe bowl in 30second intervals, stirring until smooth.

2. In a Nutribullet cup, pulse the almonds and dried cranberries until coarsely chopped.
3. Line a baking sheet with parchment paper and pour the melted chocolate onto it, spreading it evenly.
4. Sprinkle the chopped almonds and cranberries over the melted chocolate.
5. Sprinkle sea salt evenly over the top.
6. Refrigerate for at least 1 hour, or until firm.
7. Once set, break the chocolate bark into pieces and serve.

Nutritional info: Calories: 180 | Fat: 12g | Carbs: 17g | Protein: 2g

Functions used: Pulse

Nut Butter Fudge

Prep: 5 mins | Cook: 0 mins | Serves: 8

Ingredients:

- US: 1/2 cup almond butter, 1/4 cup coconut oil, melted, 2 tbsp maple syrup, 1/4 tsp vanilla extract, pinch of sea salt
- UK: 120g almond butter, 60ml coconut oil, melted, 30ml maple syrup, 1/4 tsp vanilla extract, pinch of sea salt

Instructions:

1. In a Nutribullet cup, combine the almond butter, melted coconut oil, maple syrup, vanilla extract, and sea salt.
2. Blend until smooth and creamy.
3. Pour the mixture into a parchmentlined dish and smooth the top.
4. Place in the freezer for 12 hours, or until firm.
5. Once set, cut into squares and serve.

Nutritional info: Calories: 150 | Fat: 12g | Carbs: 7g | Protein: 3g

Functions used: Blend

CHAPTER 8: MEAT AND BOWLS

Thai Quinoa Salad

Prep: 15 mins | Cook: 15 mins | Serves: 4

Ingredients:
- US: 1 cup quinoa, 2 cups water, 1 red bell pepper, chopped, 1 carrot, shredded, 1/2 cucumber, diced, 1/4 cup fresh cilantro, chopped, 1/4 cup peanuts, chopped
- UK: 200g quinoa, 480ml water, 1 red bell pepper, chopped, 1 carrot, shredded, 1/2 cucumber, diced, 15g fresh cilantro, chopped, 30g peanuts, chopped

Instructions:
1. Rinse quinoa under cold water, then cook according to package instructions.
2. In a Nutribullet cup, blend cilantro with a little water until smooth to make dressing.
3. In a large bowl, combine cooked quinoa, chopped vegetables, and cilantro dressing.
4. Toss everything together until well combined.
5. Garnish with chopped peanuts before serving.

Nutritional info: Calories: 280 | Fat: 10g | Carbs: 38g | Protein: 10g

Functions used: Blend

TexMex Rice Bowl

Prep: 10 mins | Cook: 20 mins | Serves: 4

Ingredients:
- US: 1 cup brown rice, 2 cups vegetable broth, 1 can black beans, drained and rinsed, 1 cup corn kernels, 1 avocado, diced, 1/4 cup salsa, 1/4 cup shredded cheese
- UK: 200g brown rice, 480ml vegetable broth, 1 can black beans, drained and rinsed, 150g corn kernels, 1 avocado, diced, 60ml salsa, 30g shredded cheese

Instructions:
1. Cook brown rice in vegetable broth according to package instructions.
2. In a Nutribullet cup, blend salsa until smooth.
3. In serving bowls, layer cooked rice, black beans, corn, and diced avocado.
4. Drizzle with blended salsa and sprinkle with shredded cheese.
5. Serve immediately.

Nutritional info: Calories: 320 | Fat: 12g | Carbs: 45g | Protein: 10g

Functions used: Blend

Chicken Fajita Bowl

Prep: 15 mins | Cook: 20 mins | Serves: 4

Ingredients:
- US: 1 lb chicken breast, sliced, 1 onion, sliced, 1 bell pepper, sliced, 2 tbsp olive oil, 2 tsp fajita seasoning, 1 cup cooked rice, 1/4 cup salsa, 1/4 cup sour cream
- UK: 450g chicken breast, sliced, 1 onion, sliced, 1 bell pepper, sliced, 30ml olive oil, 2 tsp fajita seasoning, 200g cooked rice, 60ml salsa, 60ml sour cream

Instructions:
1. Heat olive oil in a pan, add sliced chicken breast, onions, and bell peppers.
2. Sprinkle fajita seasoning over the chicken and vegetables. Cook until chicken is no longer pink.
3. In serving bowls, layer cooked rice with chicken fajita mixture.
4. Top with salsa and sour cream.
5. Serve hot and enjoy!

Nutritional info: Calories: 350 | Fat: 15g | Carbs: 25g | Protein: 30g

Functions used: None

Shrimp and Avocado Salad Bowl

Prep: 15 mins | Cook: 5 mins | Serves: 2

Ingredients:
- US: 1 lb shrimp, peeled and deveined, 2 cups mixed greens, 1 avocado, diced, 1/4 cup cherry tomatoes, halved, 2 tbsp olive oil, 1 tbsp lemon juice, Salt and pepper to taste
- UK: 450g shrimp, peeled and deveined, 100g mixed greens, 1 avocado, diced, 60g cherry tomatoes, halved, 30ml olive oil, 15ml lemon juice, Salt and pepper to taste

Instructions:
1. Season shrimp with salt and pepper. Cook in a pan with olive oil until pink and cooked through.
2. In a large bowl, toss mixed greens, diced avocado, and cherry tomatoes.
3. Drizzle with olive oil and lemon juice. Season with salt and pepper.
4. Top salad with cooked shrimp.
5. Serve immediately as a refreshing salad bowl.

Nutritional info: Calories: 320 | Fat: 20g | Carbs: 10g | Protein: 25g

Functions used: None

Taco Salad Bowl

Prep: 20 mins | Cook: 10 mins | Serves: 2

Ingredients:

- US: 1/2 lb ground beef, 1 cup shredded lettuce, 1/2 cup diced tomatoes, 1/4 cup diced onions, 1/4 cup shredded cheddar cheese, 1/4 cup salsa, 1/4 cup sour cream, 1/2 avocado, diced, Tortilla chips for serving
- UK: 225g ground beef, 100g shredded lettuce, 60g diced tomatoes, 30g diced onions, 30g shredded cheddar cheese, 60ml salsa, 60ml sour cream, 1/2 avocado, diced, Tortilla chips for serving

Instructions:
1. Brown ground beef in a skillet over medium heat until cooked through. Drain excess fat.
2. In a bowl, layer shredded lettuce, diced tomatoes, diced onions, and cooked ground beef.
3. Top with shredded cheddar cheese, salsa, sour cream, and diced avocado.
4. Serve with tortilla chips on the side for scooping.
5. Enjoy this TexMex delight!

Nutritional info: Calories: 420 | Fat: 25g | Carbs: 15g | Protein: 30g

Functions used: None

Curried Chickpea Salad Bowl

Prep: 15 mins | Cook: 10 mins | Serves: 2

Ingredients:
- US: 1 can chickpeas, drained and rinsed, 2 cups mixed greens, 1/2 cucumber, diced, 1/2 red bell pepper, diced, 1/4 cup diced red onion, 2 tbsp olive oil, 1 tbsp lemon juice, 1 tsp curry powder, Salt and pepper to taste
- UK: 1 can chickpeas, drained and rinsed, 100g mixed greens, 1/2 cucumber, diced, 1/2 red bell pepper, diced, 30g diced red onion, 30ml olive oil, 15ml lemon juice, 5g curry powder, Salt and pepper to taste

Instructions:
1. In a bowl, combine chickpeas, mixed greens, diced cucumber, diced red bell pepper, and diced red onion.
2. In a small bowl, whisk together olive oil, lemon juice, curry powder, salt, and pepper to make the dressing.
3. Pour the dressing over the salad and toss until well combined.
4. Serve as a nutritious and flavorful salad bowl.

Nutritional info: Calories: 320 | Fat: 15g | Carbs: 40g | Protein: 10g

Functions used: None

Vegan Chili

Prep: 15 mins | Cook: 30 mins | Serves: 4

Ingredients:
- US: 1 can (15 oz) black beans, drained and rinsed, 1 can (15 oz) kidney beans, drained and rinsed, 1 can (15 oz) diced tomatoes, 1 cup vegetable broth, 1 onion, diced, 2 cloves garlic, minced, 1 bell pepper, diced, 1 carrot, diced, 1 stalk celery, diced, 1 tbsp chili powder, 1 tsp cumin, Salt and pepper to taste
- UK: 1 can (400g) black beans, drained and rinsed, 1 can (400g) kidney beans, drained and rinsed, 1 can (400g) diced tomatoes, 240ml vegetable broth, 1 onion, diced, 2 cloves garlic, minced, 1 bell pepper, diced, 1 carrot, diced, 1 stalk celery, diced, 15g chili powder, 5g cumin, Salt and pepper to taste

Instructions:
1. In a large pot, sauté onion, garlic, bell pepper, carrot, and celery until softened.
2. Add chili powder and cumin, stirring until fragrant.
3. Pour in diced tomatoes, black beans, kidney beans, and vegetable broth.
4. Season with salt and pepper, then simmer for 2025 minutes.
5. Adjust seasoning if needed, then serve hot.

Nutritional info: Calories: 280 | Fat: 1g | Carbs: 55g | Protein: 15g

Functions used: None

Lentil Bolognese

Prep: 10 mins | Cook: 25 mins | Serves: 4

Ingredients:
- US: 1 cup lentils, rinsed, 2 cups marinara sauce, 1 onion, diced, 2 cloves garlic, minced, 1 carrot, grated, 1 stalk celery, diced, 1 tbsp olive oil, 1 tsp dried oregano, 1/2 tsp dried basil, Salt and pepper to taste
- UK: 200g lentils, rinsed, 480ml marinara sauce, 1 onion, diced, 2 cloves garlic, minced, 1 carrot, grated, 1 stalk celery, diced, 15ml olive oil, 5g dried oregano, 2.5g dried basil, Salt and pepper to taste

Instructions:
1. In a saucepan, heat olive oil over medium heat and sauté onion, garlic, carrot, and celery until softened.
2. Add lentils, marinara sauce, dried oregano, and dried basil.
3. Season with salt and pepper, then bring to a simmer.
4. Cook for 2025 minutes until lentils are tender and sauce is thickened.

5. Serve over cooked pasta or zucchini noodles.

Nutritional info: Calories: 280 | Fat: 4g | Carbs: 45g | Protein: 15g

Functions used: None

Veggie Fried Rice Bowl

Prep: 15 mins | Cook: 15 mins | Serves: 2

Ingredients:
- US: 1 cup cooked rice, 1 cup mixed vegetables (carrots, peas, corn), 2 eggs, beaten, 2 tbsp soy sauce, 1 tbsp sesame oil, 1/2 onion, diced, 2 cloves garlic, minced, 1/2 inch ginger, grated, 2 green onions, chopped, Salt and pepper to taste
- UK: 200g cooked rice, 150g mixed vegetables (carrots, peas, corn), 2 eggs, beaten, 30ml soy sauce, 15ml sesame oil, 1/2 onion, diced, 2 cloves garlic, minced, 1/2 inch ginger, grated, 2 spring onions, chopped, Salt and pepper to taste

Instructions:
1. Heat sesame oil in a pan over medium heat. Add onion, garlic, and ginger, sauté until fragrant.
2. Push vegetables to one side of the pan, pour beaten eggs into the other side. Scramble until cooked.
3. Add cooked rice and mixed vegetables to the pan. Stir to combine.
4. Pour soy sauce over the rice mixture, toss until wellcoated.
5. Season with salt and pepper, garnish with chopped green onions.

Nutritional info: Calories: 320 | Fat: 10g | Carbs: 45g | Protein: 15g

Functions used: None

Burrito Bowl

Prep: 20 mins | Cook: 20 mins | Serves: 2

Ingredients:
- US: 1 cup cooked quinoa, 1 cup black beans, cooked, 1 avocado, diced, 1/2 cup corn kernels, cooked, 1/2 cup salsa, 1/4 cup shredded cheese, 1/4 cup Greek yogurt (optional), 1 lime, cut into wedges, Fresh cilantro for garnish
- UK: 200g cooked quinoa, 200g black beans, cooked, 1 avocado, diced, 120g corn kernels, cooked, 120g salsa, 60g shredded cheese, 60g Greek yogurt (optional), 1 lime, cut into wedges, Fresh coriander for garnish

Instructions:
1. Divide cooked quinoa into serving bowls.

2. Top with black beans, diced avocado, corn kernels, salsa, and shredded cheese.
3. Add a dollop of Greek yogurt if desired.
4. Squeeze fresh lime juice over the bowl and garnish with cilantro.
5. Serve immediately.

Nutritional info: Calories: 380 | Fat: 12g | Carbs: 55g | Protein: 15g

Functions used: None

Poke Bowl

Prep: 15 mins | Cook: 0 mins | Serves: 2

Ingredients:
- US: 1 cup sushi rice, cooked, 1/2 lb sushigrade tuna, cubed, 1/2 avocado, sliced, 1/2 cup edamame, shelled, 1/2 cup cucumber, diced, 1/4 cup shredded carrots, 1/4 cup sliced radishes, 2 tbsp soy sauce, 1 tbsp sesame oil, 1 tbsp rice vinegar, 1 tsp sesame seeds, 1 green onion, chopped
- UK: 200g sushi rice, cooked, 225g sushigrade tuna, cubed, 1/2 avocado, sliced, 75g edamame, shelled, 75g cucumber, diced, 60g shredded carrots, 60g sliced radishes, 30ml soy sauce, 15ml sesame oil, 15ml rice vinegar, 5g sesame seeds, 1 spring onion, chopped

Instructions:
1. In a bowl, whisk together soy sauce, sesame oil, rice vinegar, and sesame seeds to make the sauce.
2. Divide cooked sushi rice between two bowls.
3. Arrange tuna, avocado, edamame, cucumber, shredded carrots, and sliced radishes on top of the rice.
4. Drizzle the sauce over the ingredients.
5. Garnish with chopped green onions and serve immediately.

Nutritional info: Calories: 430 | Fat: 15g | Carbs: 50g | Protein: 25g

Functions used: None

Harvest Bowl

Prep: 20 mins | Cook: 25 mins | Serves: 2

Ingredients:
- US: 1 cup quinoa, cooked, 1 sweet potato, cubed, 1 cup Brussels sprouts, halved, 1 cup cauliflower florets, 1/2 cup chickpeas, drained and rinsed, 2 tbsp olive oil, 1 tsp smoked paprika, 1/2 tsp garlic powder, Salt and pepper to taste, 2 cups baby spinach

- UK: 200g quinoa, cooked, 200g sweet potato, cubed, 150g Brussels sprouts, halved, 150g cauliflower florets, 100g chickpeas, drained and rinsed, 30ml olive oil, 5g smoked paprika, 2.5g garlic powder, Salt and pepper to taste, 100g baby spinach

Instructions:
1. Preheat the oven to 200°C (400°F).
2. Toss sweet potato cubes, Brussels sprouts, cauliflower florets, and chickpeas with olive oil, smoked paprika, garlic powder, salt, and pepper on a baking sheet.
3. Roast in the preheated oven for 25 minutes or until vegetables are tender.
4. Divide cooked quinoa and roasted vegetables between two bowls.
5. Serve over a bed of baby spinach.

Nutritional info: Calories: 380 | Fat: 12g | Carbs: 55g | Protein: 15g

Functions used: None

Tofu Scramble Bowl

Prep: 10 mins | Cook: 10 mins | Serves: 2

Ingredients:
- US: 1 block firm tofu, 2 tbsp nutritional yeast, 1/2 tsp turmeric powder, Salt and pepper to taste, 1 tbsp olive oil, 1/2 bell pepper, diced, 1/2 onion, diced, 2 cups spinach leaves
- UK: 200g firm tofu, 30g nutritional yeast, 2.5g turmeric powder, Salt and pepper to taste, 15ml olive oil, 1/2 bell pepper, diced, 1/2 onion, diced, 100g spinach leaves

Instructions:
1. Crumble the tofu into a bowl and mix in nutritional yeast, turmeric powder, salt, and pepper.
2. Heat olive oil in a skillet over medium heat.
3. Add diced bell pepper and onion to the skillet and sauté until softened.
4. Add the seasoned tofu to the skillet and cook, stirring occasionally, until heated through, about 5 minutes.
5. Add spinach leaves to the skillet and cook until wilted.
6. Divide the tofu scramble between two bowls and serve hot.

Nutritional info: Calories: 240 | Fat: 12g | Carbs: 12g | Protein: 20g

Functions used: None

Mediterranean Quinoa Salad

Prep: 15 mins | Cook: 15 mins | Serves: 4

Ingredients:
- US: 1 cup quinoa, uncooked, 1 cucumber, diced, 1 bell pepper, diced, 1/2 red onion, thinly sliced, 1 cup cherry tomatoes, halved, 1/4 cup Kalamata olives, pitted and sliced, 1/4 cup crumbled feta cheese, 1/4 cup chopped fresh parsley, 2 tbsp olive oil, 1 tbsp lemon juice, Salt and pepper to taste
- UK: 200g quinoa, uncooked, 1 cucumber, diced, 1 bell pepper, diced, 1/2 red onion, thinly sliced, 150g cherry tomatoes, halved, 30g Kalamata olives, pitted and sliced, 30g crumbled feta cheese, 15g chopped fresh parsley, 30ml olive oil, 15ml lemon juice, Salt and pepper to taste

Instructions:
1. Cook quinoa according to package instructions and let cool.
2. In a large bowl, combine cooled quinoa, diced cucumber, bell pepper, red onion, cherry tomatoes, Kalamata olives, crumbled feta cheese, and chopped parsley.
3. In a small bowl, whisk together olive oil, lemon juice, salt, and pepper to make the dressing.
4. Pour the dressing over the quinoa salad and toss to coat evenly.
5. Serve immediately or refrigerate until ready to serve.

Nutritional info: Calories: 320 | Fat: 15g | Carbs: 35g | Protein: 10g

Functions used: None

CHAPTER 9: DRINKS

Nutribullet Milkshakes

Prep: 5 mins | Cook: 0 mins | Serves: 2

Ingredients:
- US: 2 cups vanilla ice cream, 1 cup milk, 1 tsp vanilla extract, 2 tbsp chocolate syrup
- UK: 300g vanilla ice cream, 240ml milk, 5ml vanilla extract, 30ml chocolate syrup

Instructions:
1. Place vanilla ice cream, milk, and vanilla extract in the Nutribullet cup.
2. Blend on high speed until smooth and creamy.
3. Drizzle chocolate syrup inside serving glasses.
4. Pour the milkshake into the glasses and serve immediately.

Nutritional info: Calories: 300 | Fat: 12g | Carbs: 40g | Protein: 8g

Functions used: Blending

Fruit Smoothies

Prep: 5 mins | Cook: 0 mins | Serves: 2

Ingredients:
- US: 1 cup mixed frozen fruits (berries, mango, pineapple), 1 banana, 1 cup orange juice
- UK: 150g mixed frozen fruits (berries, mango, pineapple), 1 banana, 240ml orange juice

Instructions:
1. Add mixed frozen fruits, banana, and orange juice into the Nutribullet cup.
2. Blend on high speed until smooth.
3. Pour into glasses and serve immediately.

Nutritional info: Calories: 150 | Fat: 0.5g | Carbs: 38g | Protein: 2g

Functions used: Blending

Green Juice

Prep: 5 mins | Cook: 0 mins | Serves: 1

Ingredients:
- US: 2 cups spinach, 1 cucumber, 1 green apple, 1 lemon (juiced), 1inch piece of ginger
- UK: 60g spinach, 1 cucumber, 1 green apple, 1 lemon (juiced), 2.5cm piece of ginger

Instructions:
1. Wash and chop the spinach, cucumber, and green apple.

2. Add all ingredients into the Nutribullet cup.
3. Blend until smooth.
4. Strain the juice using a fine mesh sieve if desired.

Nutritional info: Calories: 120 | Fat: 0.5g | Carbs: 30g | Protein: 3g

Functions used: Blending

Nutribullet Lattes

Prep: 5 mins | Cook: 5 mins | Serves: 1

Ingredients:
- US: 1 cup brewed coffee, 1/2 cup milk, 1 tbsp sugar, 1/2 tsp vanilla extract
- UK: 240ml brewed coffee, 120ml milk, 15g sugar, 2.5ml vanilla extract

Instructions:
1. Brew coffee and heat milk.
2. Pour coffee, hot milk, sugar, and vanilla extract into the Nutribullet cup.
3. Blend until frothy.
4. Pour into a mug and serve hot.

Nutritional info: Calories: 80 | Fat: 1g | Carbs: 14g | Protein: 3g

Functions used: Blending, heating

Matcha Latte

Prep: 5 mins | Cook: 5 mins | Serves: 1

Ingredients:
- US: 1 tsp matcha powder, 1 cup milk, 1 tbsp honey
- UK: 5g matcha powder, 240ml milk, 15g honey

Instructions:
1. Heat milk until hot but not boiling.
2. Add matcha powder and honey into the Nutribullet cup.
3. Pour in hot milk.
4. Blend until frothy.
5. Pour into a mug and serve hot.

Nutritional info: Calories: 130 | Fat: 2g | Carbs: 20g | Protein: 7g

Functions used: Blending, heating

Pumpkin Spice Latte

Prep: 5 mins | Cook: 5 mins | Serves: 1

Ingredients:
- US: 1 cup brewed coffee, 1/2 cup milk, 2 tbsp pumpkin puree, 1 tbsp maple syrup, 1/2 tsp pumpkin pie spice
- UK: 240ml brewed coffee, 120ml milk, 30g pumpkin puree, 15ml maple syrup, 2.5ml pumpkin pie spice

Instructions:
1. Brew coffee and heat milk.
2. Add brewed coffee, hot milk, pumpkin puree, maple syrup, and pumpkin pie spice to the Nutribullet cup.
3. Blend until smooth and frothy.
4. Pour into a mug and serve hot.

Nutritional info: Calories: 130 | Fat: 1g | Carbs: 26g | Protein: 5g

Functions used: Blending, heating

Iced Mocha Latte

Prep: 5 mins | Cook: 0 mins | Serves: 1

Ingredients:
- US: 1 cup brewed coffee, 1/2 cup milk, 2 tbsp chocolate syrup, ice cubes
- UK: 240ml brewed coffee, 120ml milk, 30ml chocolate syrup, ice cubes

Instructions:
1. Brew coffee and let it cool.
2. Add brewed coffee, milk, and chocolate syrup to the Nutribullet cup.
3. Blend until well combined.
4. Fill a glass with ice cubes and pour the mixture over it.
5. Stir and serve chilled.

Nutritional info: Calories: 120 | Fat: 2g | Carbs: 22g | Protein: 3g

Functions used: Blending

Golden Milk Turmeric Latte

Prep: 5 mins | Cook: 5 mins | Serves: 1

Ingredients:
- US: 1 cup milk, 1 tsp turmeric powder, 1/2 tsp cinnamon, 1/4 tsp ginger powder, 1 tbsp honey
- UK: 240ml milk, 5g turmeric powder, 2.5ml cinnamon, 1.25ml ginger powder, 15ml honey

Instructions:
1. Heat milk until hot but not boiling.
2. Add turmeric powder, cinnamon, ginger powder, and honey to the Nutribullet cup.
3. Pour in hot milk.
4. Blend until frothy.
5. Pour into a mug and serve hot.

Nutritional info: Calories: 120 | Fat: 1g | Carbs: 25g | Protein: 5g

Functions used: Blending, heating

Hot Chocolate

Prep: 5 mins | Cook: 5 mins | Serves: 1

Ingredients:
- US: 1 cup milk, 2 tbsp cocoa powder, 1 tbsp sugar, whipped cream (optional)
- UK: 240ml milk, 30g cocoa powder, 15g sugar, whipped cream (optional)

Instructions:
1. Heat milk until hot but not boiling.
2. Add cocoa powder and sugar to the Nutribullet cup.
3. Pour in hot milk.
4. Blend until smooth and frothy.
5. Pour into a mug, top with whipped cream if desired, and serve hot.

Nutritional info: Calories: 150 | Fat: 2g | Carbs: 28g | Protein: 7g

Functions used: Blending, heating

Chai Latte

Prep: 5 mins | Cook: 5 mins | Serves: 1

Ingredients:
- US: 1 cup milk, 1 black tea bag, 1/2 tsp ground cinnamon, 1/4 tsp ground ginger, 1/4 tsp ground cardamom, 1 tbsp honey

- UK: 240ml milk, 1 black tea bag, 2.5ml ground cinnamon, 1.25ml ground ginger, 1.25ml ground cardamom, 15ml honey

Instructions:
1. Heat milk until hot but not boiling.
2. Steep the black tea bag in the hot milk for 35 minutes.
3. Remove the tea bag and add ground cinnamon, ginger, cardamom, and honey to the Nutribullet cup.
4. Pour in the steeped milk.
5. Blend until well combined and frothy.
6. Pour into a mug and serve hot.

Nutritional info: Calories: 140 | Fat: 2g | Carbs: 27g | Protein: 7g

Functions used: Blending, steeping

Strawberry Banana Smoothie

Prep: 5 mins | Cook: 0 mins | Serves: 1

Ingredients:
- US: 1 banana, 1/2 cup strawberries, 1/2 cup milk, 1/2 cup yogurt, 1 tbsp honey
- UK: 1 banana, 120g strawberries, 120ml milk, 120ml yogurt, 15ml honey

Instructions:
1. Peel the banana and wash the strawberries.
2. Add banana, strawberries, milk, yogurt, and honey to the Nutribullet cup.
3. Blend until smooth.
4. Pour into a glass and serve immediately.

Nutritional info: Calories: 200 | Fat: 2g | Carbs: 40g | Protein: 8g

Functions used: Blending

Peanut Butter Banana Protein Shake

Prep: 5 mins | Cook: 0 mins | Serves: 1

Ingredients:
- US: 1 banana, 1 tbsp peanut butter, 1/2 cup milk, 1/2 cup Greek yogurt, 1 scoop protein powder
- UK: 1 banana, 15g peanut butter, 120ml milk, 120ml Greek yogurt, 1 scoop protein powder

Instructions:
1. Peel the banana.
2. Add banana, peanut butter, milk, Greek yogurt, and protein powder to the Nutribullet cup.

3. Blend until smooth.
4. Pour into a glass and serve immediately.

Nutritional info: Calories: 320 | Fat: 8g | Carbs: 40g | Protein: 26g

Functions used: Blending

Blueberry Almond Smoothie

Prep: 5 mins | Cook: 0 mins | Serves: 1

Ingredients:
- US: 1/2 cup blueberries, 1/4 cup almonds, 1/2 cup spinach, 1/2 banana, 1/2 cup almond milk, 1 tbsp honey
- UK: 60g blueberries, 30g almonds, 60g spinach, 1/2 banana, 120ml almond milk, 15ml honey

Instructions:
1. Rinse the blueberries and spinach.
2. Add blueberries, almonds, spinach, banana, almond milk, and honey to the Nutribullet cup.
3. Blend until smooth.
4. Pour into a glass and serve immediately.

Nutritional info: Calories: 290 | Fat: 13g | Carbs: 40g | Protein: 9g

Functions used: Blending

Watermelon Juice

Prep: 5 mins | Cook: 0 mins | Serves: 1

Ingredients:
- US: 2 cups diced watermelon, 1/2 lime (juiced), 1/4 cup cold water, Ice cubes
- UK: 480ml diced watermelon, Juice of 1/2 lime, 60ml cold water, Ice cubes

Instructions:
1. Remove the seeds from the watermelon and dice it.
2. Juice the lime.
3. Add diced watermelon, lime juice, cold water, and ice cubes to the Nutribullet cup.
4. Blend until smooth.
5. Pour into a glass and serve chilled.

Nutritional info: Calories: 90 | Fat: 0g | Carbs: 22g | Protein: 2g

Functions used: Blending

Orange Juice

Prep: 5 mins | Cook: 0 mins | Serves: 1

Ingredients:
- US: 2 large oranges, 1/4 cup cold water, Ice cubes
- UK: 2 large oranges, 60ml cold water, Ice cubes

Instructions:
1. Peel the oranges and remove any seeds.
2. Add peeled oranges, cold water, and ice cubes to the Nutribullet cup.
3. Blend until smooth.
4. Pour into a glass and serve chilled.

Nutritional info: Calories: 110 | Fat: 0g | Carbs: 27g | Protein: 2g

Functions used: Blending

CHAPTER 10: NUTRIBULLET TIPS AND RESOURCES

Substituting Ingredients:

One of the great things about the NutriBullet is its versatility. The recipes in this book are designed to be flexible, allowing you to swap out ingredients based on your personal preferences, dietary needs, and what's available in your kitchen.

When it comes to substitutions, think about the overall flavor profile and texture you're going for. For example, if a recipe calls for almond milk, you could easily substitute another nondairy milk like oat, cashew, or coconut milk. Or if a smoothie recipe includes banana, you could swap in another creamy fruit like avocado or mango.

Don't be afraid to get creative with your substitutions. Try swapping out leafy greens, using different nuts and seeds, or experimenting with various spices and herbs. The NutriBullet makes it easy to blend up something new and delicious every time.

Just keep a few key things in mind:

Stick to similar textures and consistencies to maintain the desired mouthfeel. For example, substituting applesauce for bananas may result in a thinner consistency.

Be mindful of dietary restrictions or allergies when making substitutions. Avoid ingredients that may cause an adverse reaction.

Consider how the new ingredient will impact the overall flavor profile. Substituting an acidic fruit like pineapple for a sweet banana, for instance, will result in a tangier smoothie.

With a little experimentation, you'll quickly get the hang of making substitutions that work for your taste buds and nutritional needs. The possibilities are truly endless when you have the power of the NutriBullet at your fingertips.

Freezing and Storing Smoothies

One of the best things about the NutriBullet is how it allows you to quickly and easily blend up nutrient dense smoothies anytime. But what if you want to make your smoothies in advance or save leftovers for later? No problem the NutriBullet makes it easy to freeze and store your creations for optimal freshness and convenience.

When freezing smoothies, it's best to pour the blended mixture into individual servingsized containers or ice cube trays. This will allow you to thaw and enjoy just the right amount whenever a smoothie craving strikes. Mason jars, reusable silicone bags, or BPAfree plastic containers all work great for this purpose.

Be sure to leave a bit of headspace at the top of your containers to account for expansion during freezing. It's also a good idea to write the contents and date on the outside so you can easily keep track of your stash.

Most smoothie ingredients will retain their nutrients and flavor when frozen, but there are a few tips to keep in mind:

 Avoid freezing smoothies with fresh leafy greens like spinach or kale, as they can become bitter and oxidize more quickly in the freezer. Instead, use frozen greens or wait to add fresh greens when reheating or blending.

 Nut butters, avocado, and bananas can also change in texture and flavor when frozen. You may want to omit these ingredients or blend them in fresh when ready to enjoy.

 Dairy based ingredients like yogurt or milk may separate or curdle when frozen and thawed. If using these, it's best to blend them in fresh.

When you're ready to enjoy your frozen smoothie, simply transfer the container to the refrigerator the night before or thaw it at room temperature for 3060 minutes. Then give it a quick reblend in your NutriBullet to restore the smooth, creamy texture.

Storing unfrozen smoothies can be a bit trickier, as the natural sugars and enzymes in the fruit can cause the mixture to ferment and spoil over time. For best results, consume your freshly blended smoothie within 2448 hours. If you know you won't finish it right away, remove the easy twist extractor blade, cover the container with plastic wrap, and refrigerate.

With a little planning and preparation, you can always have a nutritious, delicious smoothie on hand whether you're blending it fresh or thawing from the freezer. The NutriBullet makes it easy to enjoy the benefits of whole food nutrition any time of day.

Variations for Dietary Needs

One of the most powerful aspects of the NutriBullet is its ability to support a wide range of dietary needs and preferences. Whether you're following a vegan, paleo, keto, or glutenfree lifestyle, the NutriBullet can be tailored to suit your nutritional requirements.

Let's take a look at some simple substitutions and adjustments you can make to adapt the recipes in this book:

Vegan/Vegetarian:

Swap out dairybased milk, yogurt, and cheese for plantbased alternatives like almond, oat, or coconut milk, plantbased yogurt, and nutritional yeast.

Replace eggs with mashed banana, applesauce, or commercial egg replacer.

Use nut or seed butters instead of dairybased protein powders.

Load up on nutrientdense plantbased ingredients like leafy greens, berries, avocado, and chia/flax seeds.

Paleo:

Avoid grains, legumes, and dairy. Stick to whole foods like vegetables, fruits, nuts, seeds, and healthy fats.

Use nut or coconut milk as a base instead of dairy.

Sweeten with honey, maple syrup, or fruit instead of added sugars.

Incorporate paleofriendly proteins like grassfed collagen, egg whites, or nut/seed butters.

Keto:

Focus on healthy fats like avocado, coconut oil, nut butters, and MCT oil.

Use lowcarb fruits like berries, lemon, and lime.

Avoid highcarb ingredients like bananas, honey, and most dairy.

Utilize ketoapproved sweeteners like stevia, monk fruit, or erythritol.

Include MCT oil, chia seeds, and fullfat coconut milk for an extra fat boost.

GlutenFree:

Substitute glutenfree oats or nut flours for regular wheatbased flour.

Avoid ingredients containing gluten, such as wheat, barley, rye, and some oats.

Choose glutenfree grains like quinoa, buckwheat, and certified glutenfree oats.

Use tamari or coconut aminos instead of soy sauce.

No matter your dietary needs, the versatility of the NutriBullet allows you to create delicious, nutrientdense recipes that fit your lifestyle. Don't be afraid to experiment and find the combinations that work best for you.

Remember, the key is to focus on whole, unprocessed ingredients that provide a balance of protein, healthy fats, complex carbs, and fiber. With a little creativity and the power of the NutriBullet, you can enjoy flavorful, satisfying meals and snacks that support your overall health and wellness.

Keeping it Simple

One of the best things about the NutriBullet is how easy it makes it to incorporate more whole, nutrientdense foods into your daily routine. However, with so many delicious recipe options at your fingertips, it can be tempting to overcomplicate things.

The truth is, some of the most nourishing and satisfying NutriBullet creations are the simplest ones. By focusing on highquality, whole food ingredients and mastering a few essential techniques, you can whip up flavorful and nutritious meals and snacks with minimal effort.

Here are a few tips for keeping it simple with your NutriBullet:

1. Start with a Solid Base

Whether you're making a smoothie, soup, or sauce, begin with a liquid base that provides a smooth, creamy texture. This could be anything from nondairy milk and yogurt to broth and nut butters. The liquid base helps everything blend together seamlessly.

2. Load up on NutrientDense Produce

Fruits and vegetables are the foundation of so many NutriBullet recipes. Focus on incorporating a variety of fresh, seasonal produce that provides a wealth of vitamins, minerals, and antioxidants. Leafy greens, berries, and tropical fruits are all excellent options.

3. Customize with Healthy Fats and Proteins

To make your NutriBullet creations more filling and satisfying, add in a source of healthy fat (such as avocado, nuts, or nut butter) and a proteinrich ingredient (like Greek yogurt, silken tofu, or collagen powder). These additions will help balance your blood sugar and keep you energized.

4. Embrace Simple Seasonings

Don't feel like you need to overload your recipes with a long list of spices and herbs. Sometimes, the beauty is in the simplicity. A sprinkle of cinnamon, a squeeze of citrus, or a dash of vanilla can go a long way in enhancing the natural flavors of your ingredients.

5. Batch Prep for Convenience

Setting aside some time on the weekend to prep ingredients or preportion smoothie ingredients into individual servings can save you a ton of time during the busy workweek. That way, you can quickly blend and enjoy a nutrientdense meal or snack anytime.

Remember, the NutriBullet is all about making healthy eating easy and accessible. Don't feel like you need to reinvent the wheel with every recipe. Sometimes, the most nourishing and delicious creations come from embracing simplicity and letting the quality of your ingredients shine.

Portion Sizes

One of the great things about the NutriBullet is how it encourages you to focus on nutrientdense whole foods. However, it's important to be mindful of portion sizes to ensure you're getting the right balance of nutrients and calories.

When it comes to smoothies, it's easy to get carried away and end up with a serving that's much larger than what our bodies actually need. While smoothies are a fantastic way to pack a nutritional punch, it's important to consume them in moderation as part of an overall balanced diet.

As a general guideline, aim for a smoothie portion size of 1216 ounces. This provides enough volume to feel satisfied, while still maintaining a sensible calorie and nutrient profile. If you find yourself consistently craving or needing a larger portion, consider adding more fiberrich ingredients like leafy greens, chia seeds, or oats to help keep you fuller for longer.

For other NutriBullet recipes, such as sauces, dips, and nut butters, pay attention to the serving size recommendations in the recipes. These nutrientdense creations are meant to be enjoyed in smaller portions, often as a complement to larger meals or as a satisfying snack.

When building your NutriBullet recipes, be mindful of using caloriedense ingredients like nut butters, avocado, and coconut in moderation. A little goes a long way in terms of adding healthy fats, creaminess, and flavor.

It's also a good idea to listen to your body's hunger and fullness cues. If you find yourself feeling overly full or experiencing digestive discomfort after a NutriBullet creation, try reducing the portion size or adjusting the ingredient ratios next time.

Remember, the NutriBullet is all about nourishing your body with whole, nutrientdense foods. By keeping portion sizes in check, you can enjoy all the benefits of these delicious and healthy recipes without any undesirable side effects.

Choosing Your Ingredients

One of the keys to unlocking the full potential of your NutriBullet is choosing highquality, nutrientdense ingredients. The better the quality of your produce, nuts, seeds, and other addins, the more nourishing and delicious your final creations will be.

When shopping for NutriBullet ingredients, prioritize the following:

Organic Produce

Whenever possible, opt for organic fruits and vegetables. This helps minimize your exposure to harmful pesticides and ensures you're getting the maximum nutritional value from your produce.

InSeason Produce

Choosing fruits and veggies that are inseason not only ensures optimal freshness and flavor, but it also supports local farmers and the environment. Plus, seasonal produce is often more affordable.

Frozen Fruits and Veggies

Frozen produce can be just as nutritious as fresh, and it's a great way to enjoy your favorite fruits and veggies yearround. Look for bags that contain only the produce itself, without any added sugars or preservatives.

HighQuality Nuts and Seeds

Invest in raw, unsalted nuts and seeds that are free from additives or rancid oils. These nutrientdense ingredients will lend a delicious, satisfying crunch to your NutriBullet creations.

Healthy Fats

Incorporate hearthealthy fats like avocado, coconut oil, olive oil, and nut and seed butters. These nutrientrich additions will help keep you feeling full and satisfied.

PlantBased Milk Alternatives

Skip the dairy and opt for nondairy milk options like almond, oat, coconut, or cashew milk. They're a great way to add creaminess and essential nutrients to your smoothies and other recipes.

Organic Herbs and Spices

Elevate the flavor of your NutriBullet dishes with fresh or dried herbs and spices. Look for organic, pesticidefree varieties to get the most out of their aromatic and medicinal properties.

By prioritizing highquality, whole food ingredients, you'll not only create more delicious and nutrientdense recipes, but you'll also be supporting your overall health and wellness in the process.

Remember, the NutriBullet is all about unlocking the power of real, unprocessed foods. With a little intentionality in your ingredient selection, you can maximize the benefits of this amazing kitchen tool.

Adding Protein and Fiber

When it comes to creating satisfying and nourishing NutriBullet recipes, two key components to focus on are protein and fiber. These essential nutrients play a vital role in keeping you feeling full, energized, and supporting overall health.

Protein is the building block of our cells, helping to repair and maintain muscle, bone, and tissue. It also plays a crucial role in regulating hormone function, boosting immunity, and stabilizing blood sugar levels. By incorporating protein rich ingredients into your NutriBullet creations, you can help keep hunger at bay and support your body's natural processes.

Some great protein packed additions for your NutriBullet recipes include:

Plant based proteins like nut and seed butters, silken tofu, and plant based protein powders.

Dairy based proteins like Greek yogurt, cottage cheese, and whey or casein powder Collagen peptides, which provide amino acids to support skin, hair, nails, and joint health

Fiber, on the other hand, is essential for maintaining a healthy digestive system and promoting feelings of fullness. Soluble fiber helps slow the absorption of nutrients, while insoluble fiber adds bulk to stool and prevents constipation. Both types of fiber offer a wealth of other benefits, from stabilizing blood sugar to reducing cholesterol levels.

Excellent fiber rich ingredients to blend into your NutriBullet recipes include:

- Chia seeds, flaxseeds, and ground flaxseed
- Oats, oat bran, and whole grains
- Berries, leafy greens, and other fruits and veggies
- Psyllium husk and wheat germ

When adding protein and fiber to your NutriBullet creations, start with small amounts and gradually increase based on your personal needs and preferences. Pay attention to how your body responds, and don't be afraid to experiment to find the right balance.

By thoughtfully incorporating these essential nutrients, you can transform your NutriBullet recipes into satisfying, nutrientdense meals and snacks that will keep you feeling your best. Whether you're blending up a smoothie, whipping up a nut butter, or crafting a savory spread, protein and fiber are sure to take your creations to the next level.

Blending Tips

Mastering the art of blending with your NutriBullet is key to unlocking its full potential. By following a few simple tips and techniques, you can ensure your NutriBullet creations turn out perfectly smooth, consistent, and nutrientdense every time.

First and foremost, always start by adding your liquid ingredients to the NutriBullet cup or pitcher. This helps ensure even distribution and prevents ingredients from getting stuck at the bottom. Gradually add your solid ingredients, making sure not to overfill the vessel.

When blending, begin on a lower speed and gradually increase as needed. This gentle approach helps preserve the delicate nutrients in your ingredients. Avoid running the NutriBullet for more than 60 seconds at a time excessive friction can cause ingredients to heat up. If you need to blend for longer, allow the motor to rest for a minute or two between cycles.

Finally, don't be afraid to use the tamper tool to gently guide ingredients toward the blades. This helps ensure everything gets thoroughly incorporated without overworking the motor. With a little practice, you'll be blending like a pro in no time!

Smoothie Prep and Storage Ideas

One of the best things about the NutriBullet is how it streamlines the process of making nutritious smoothies. With just a few minutes of prep work, you can have a delicious, nutrientdense beverage ready to enjoy anytime. And by taking advantage of some smart storage strategies, you can ensure your smoothies stay fresh and ready to blend at a moment's notice.

To get started, try batch prepping your smoothie ingredients ahead of time. Measure out your fruits, veggies, nut butters, and other addins into individual servingsized portions, then store them in the freezer in airtight containers or reusable silicone bags. That way, all you have to do is grab a preportioned pack, add your liquid base, and blend. This makes for super quick and easy smoothie assembly on busy mornings.

For an even bigger timesaver, you can also preblend your smoothies and then freeze them in individual servings. Simply pour the blended mixture into ice cube trays or small containers, let them freeze, then pop the cubes out and store them in a larger freezersafe bag or container. When a smoothie craving strikes, just grab a few frozen cubes, add your liquid, and reblend for a refreshing, nutrientdense treat.

No matter which smoothie prep method you choose, be sure to consume your blended creations within 2448 hours for optimal freshness and nutrient retention. With a little advance planning, the NutriBullet makes it a breeze to enjoy wholesome, delicious smoothies anytime.

Creative Vessels and Toppings

While the classic NutriBullet cups are undoubtedly convenient for blending and enjoying your creations on the go, don't be afraid to think outside the box when it comes to serving vessels. Experimenting with different containers can not only add a fun, Instagramworthy flair to your recipes, but it can also enhance the overall experience.

For smoothie bowls, try pouring your blended creation into a shallow bowl or even a widerimmed plate. This allows you to get creative with fun toppings like sliced fruit, toasted nuts and seeds, shredded coconut, and a drizzle of nut butter or honey. The possibilities are endless! You can even serve your smoothie bowl in a halved avocado or coconut shell for a unique presentation.

When blending sauces, dips, and spreads, consider transferring them to small ramekins or mason jars. Not only do these vessels look adorable, but they also make for easy dipping and portioning. Serve your Nutribullet hummus or guacamole with carrot sticks, cucumber slices, or whole grain crackers for a satisfying and visually appealing snack.

For a touch of elegance, try pouring your Nutribullet creations into delicate teacups or small glasses. This works beautifully for puddings, custards, and even mini smoothie shooters. Top them off with a sprinkle of cinnamon, a fresh mint sprig, or a dollop of whipped cream for a truly indulgent treat.

The beauty of the Nutribullet is that it empowers you to get creative in the kitchen. By thinking beyond the standard cups and glasses, you can elevate your recipes and turn them into edible works of art.

Tips

Safety should always be a top priority when using your Nutribullet. While this powerful blender makes it easy to create nutrientdense meals and snacks, it's important to follow proper safety precautions to avoid any potential hazards. Here are some key safety tips to keep in mind when operating your Nutribullet:

Never blend hot ingredients in a sealed Nutribullet cup. The friction from the blades combined with the thermal energy of the hot contents can create dangerous pressure buildup, potentially causing the cup and blade to separate violently. Always start with room temperature or refrigerated ingredients, and never continuously blend for more than 1 minute at a time to prevent overheating.

When blending hot liquids, such as soups or sauces, use the Nutribullet pitcher with the vented lid cap locked in place. This allows steam and pressure to escape safely, guarding against excessive splashing or eruption. Never attempt to blend hot items in a sealed container.

Exercise caution when handling the sharp blades, and never touch the blades directly. If you need to dislodge ingredients, use the tamper tool provided never insert your hands or other utensils into the cup or pitcher while the blender is in use.

Always ensure the Nutribullet is properly assembled before blending, and never leave the machine unattended while it's running. When you're finished blending, allow the motor to come to a complete stop before removing the cup or pitcher.

By following these simple safety guidelines, you can enjoy all the benefits of your Nutribullet while prioritizing your wellbeing. Stay vigilant, blend with care, and your Nutribullet will serve you well on your health and wellness journey.

Cleaning the Nutribullet

Proper cleaning and maintenance is essential for keeping your Nutribullet in top working condition and ensuring optimal performance. Luckily, the Nutribullet is designed with easytoclean components that make the postblending cleanup a breeze.

Start by unplugging the motor base and disassembling the Nutribullet remove the cup or pitcher, as well as the easytwist extractor blade or pitcher lid. This will give you full access to each component for thorough cleaning.

The Nutribullet cups and togo lids are toprack dishwasher safe, making them a cinch to clean. For best results, give them a quick rinse or light scrub with a dish brush before placing them in the dishwasher. Avoid using the sanitize cycle, as the high heat can potentially warp the plastic.

When it comes to the easytwist extractor blade, take extra care as the blades are sharp. It's best to clean the blade immediately after use to prevent the buildup of dried, stubborn ingredients. Use a small brush or sponge to gently scrub the blades, being mindful not to touch the sharp edges. Avoid submerging the entire blade assembly in water, as this can damage the internal components.

For the motor base, wipe down the exterior with a damp cloth or sponge. Pay close attention to the area around the blade coupling, making sure to remove any stuckon debris. Never submerge the motor base in water, as this can lead to electrical damage.

By following these simple cleaning steps after each use, you'll keep your Nutribullet running smoothly and ensure it continues to deliver powerful, nutrientdense blends for years to come.

Top Resources and Websites

As you embark on your Nutribullet journey, there's a wealth of information and inspiration available to help you get the most out of your machine. From recipe ideas to blending tips and nutritional guidance, these top resources and websites are sure to become invaluable tools in your wellness arsenal.

First and foremost, be sure to visit the official Nutribullet website at nutribullet.com. Here you'll find a comprehensive library of Nutribullet recipes covering everything from smoothies and juices to nut butters and dips. The site also offers helpful howto guides, troubleshooting tips, and information on the latest Nutribullet models and accessories.

For an even deeper dive into the world of Nutribullet blending, check out the official Nutribullet app, available for both iOS and Android devices. This app puts thousands of curated recipes right at your fingertips, along with meal planning tools, shopping lists, and video tutorials to walk you through various blending techniques.

Looking to take your Nutribullet creations to the next level? Explore the vibrant community of Nutribullet enthusiasts on social media platforms like Instagram, Facebook, and YouTube. These channels are brimming with mouthwatering recipe ideas, blending hacks, and firsthand user experiences to inspire your own culinary adventures.

Finally, be sure to bookmark trusted health and nutrition websites like WebMD, the Mayo Clinic, and the Academy of Nutrition and Dietetics. These resources can provide valuable guidance on selecting the right ingredients, understanding nutritional information, and incorporating the Nutribullet into an overall healthy lifestyle.

With so many incredible tools and communities at your fingertips, you'll never run out of ways to optimize your Nutribullet experience. Dive in, get inspired, and enjoy the journey towards better health and wellness.

CONCLUSION

As you've discovered throughout the pages of this Nutribullet Recipe Book, the possibilities for creating delicious, nutrientdense meals and snacks are truly endless. From classic fruit smoothies to innovative vegetablepacked blends, the Nutribullet has the power to transform the way you approach your health and wellness goals.

Through the unique process of nutrient extraction, the Nutribullet allows you to harness the full nutritional potential of whole foods, making it easier for your body to absorb vitamins, minerals, and phytonutrients. This not only supports overall health and vitality, but can also provide targeted benefits like increased energy, improved digestion, and reduced inflammation.

But the Nutribullet is about more than just the end result it's about the journey towards better habits and a more nourishing lifestyle. By incorporating the Nutribullet into your daily routine, you'll find that it becomes an indispensable tool for quickly and easily incorporating more fruits, vegetables, and other whole, unprocessed ingredients into your diet.

Whether you're looking to start your day with a nutrientdense smoothie, fuel your body after a workout, or satisfy a sweet craving with a guiltfree dessert, the recipes in this book have you covered. And the beauty of the Nutribullet is that you can easily customize these recipes to suit your personal tastes and dietary needs.

Not a fan of spinach? Swap it for kale. Allergic to nuts? Try using seeds instead. The Nutribullet makes it easy to experiment and find the flavor combinations that work best for you.

Of course, with great power comes great responsibility. As you continue on your Nutribullet journey, it's important to keep safety top of mind. Always follow the manufacturer's instructions, avoid blending hot liquids in sealed containers, and handle the sharp blades with care. By prioritizing safety, you can enjoy all the benefits of your Nutribullet without any unwanted surprises.

And speaking of benefits, the longterm advantages of incorporating the Nutribullet into your lifestyle are truly remarkable. By making nutrientdense smoothies, juices, and other blended creations a regular part of your routine, you're investing in your overall health and wellbeing in a tangible way.

Increased energy, improved digestion, better skin and hair these are just a few of the potential dividends you may reap. And as you continue to experiment with new ingredients and flavor combinations, you'll find that the Nutribullet becomes an indispensable tool for supporting your specific health and wellness goals.

Perhaps you're looking to shed a few pounds through a more plantbased, fiberrich diet. Or maybe you're aiming to boost your immune system and stave off seasonal illnesses. Whatever your motivation, the Nutribullet has the versatility to help you achieve your objectives, one delicious blend at a time.

Of course, the Nutribullet is just one piece of the puzzle. For lasting, transformative change, it's important to pair your Nutribullet habits with other healthy lifestyle choices, such as regular exercise, stress management, and quality sleep. But by making the Nutribullet a cornerstone of your wellness routine, you'll be well on your way to feeling your absolute best.

So as you close this book and turn your attention to the Nutribullet waiting on your kitchen counter, I encourage you to approach it with a sense of excitement and possibility. This machine has the power to unlock a world of vibrant, nutrientdense flavors and with a little creativity and experimentation, you'll be whipping up blends that nourish your body and delight your taste buds.

Remember, the journey is just as important as the destination. Embrace the process of discovery, celebrate your successes, and don't be afraid to get a little messy along the way. With the Nutribullet as your guide, the path to better health and wellness has never been more delicious.

So, what are you waiting for? It's time to get blending!

Printed in Great Britain
by Amazon